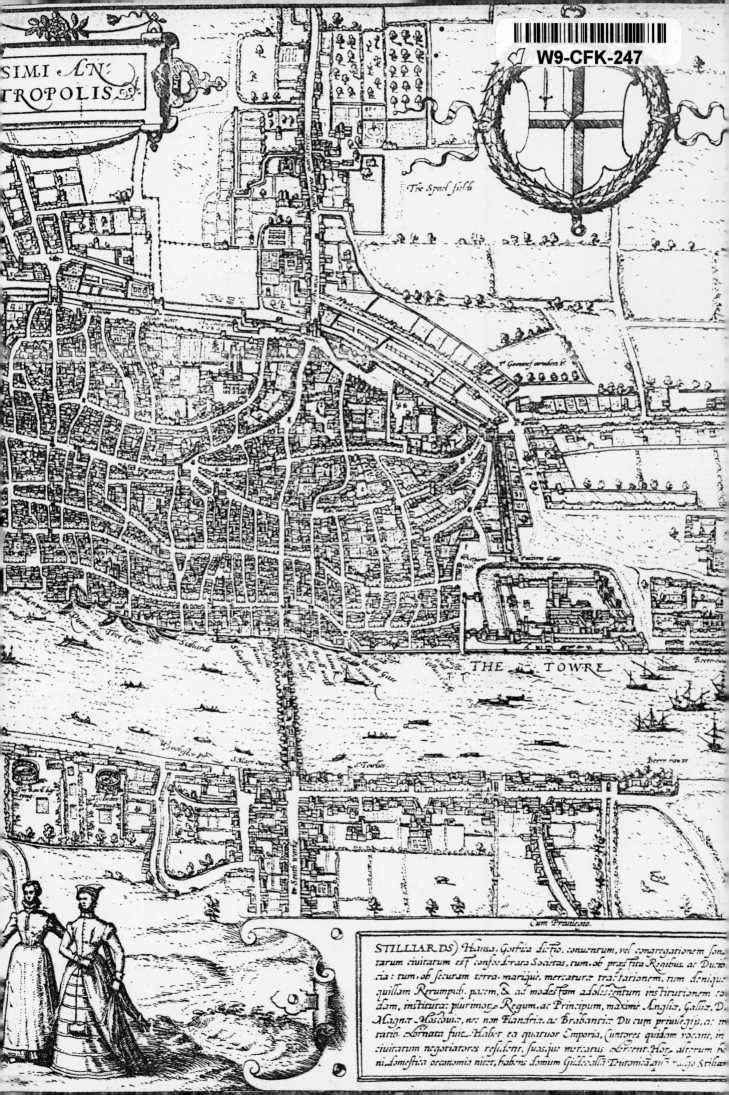

SIMI AN-
TROPOLIS

The Spul fields

THE TOWRE

STILLIARDS) Hansa, Gothica dictio, conuentum, vel congregationem son-
tarum ciuitatum est confaederata Societas, tum ob praefita Regibus, ac Du-
cia: tum, ob securam terra, marique, mercatura tractationem, tum deniq;
quillam Rerumpub. pacem, & ad modestam adolescentum institutionem co
dam, instituta: plurimorq; Regum, ac Principum, maxime Angliae, Galliae, D.
Magnae Moscouiae, nec non Flandriae, ac Brabantiae Ducum priuilegijs, ac
ratib. Jornata sunt. Habet ea quatuor Emporia, Cuntores quidam vocant, in
ciuitatum negotiatores resident, suasque mercatus exercent. Hor, alterum b
ni, domestica oeconomia nitet, habens domum Gildehalla Teutonica auc vulgo Stillia

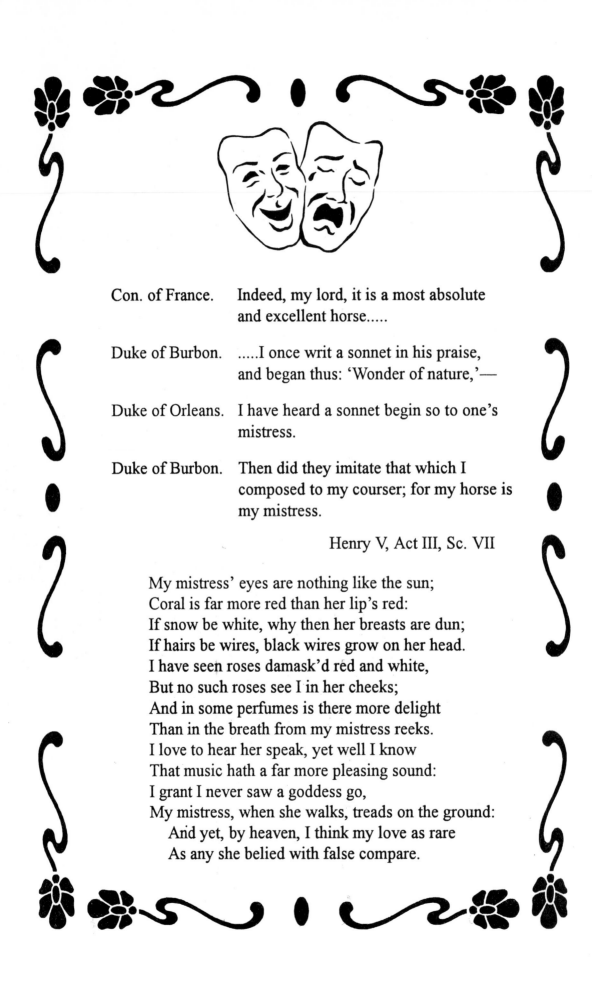

Con. of France.   Indeed, my lord, it is a most absolute
and excellent horse.....

Duke of Burbon.   .....I once writ a sonnet in his praise,
and began thus: 'Wonder of nature,'—

Duke of Orleans.   I have heard a sonnet begin so to one's
mistress.

Duke of Burbon.   Then did they imitate that which I
composed to my courser; for my horse is
my mistress.

Henry V, Act III, Sc. VII

My mistress' eyes are nothing like the sun;
Coral is far more red than her lip's red:
If snow be white, why then her breasts are dun;
If hairs be wires, black wires grow on her head.
I have seen roses damask'd red and white,
But no such roses see I in her cheeks;
And in some perfumes is there more delight
Than in the breath from my mistress reeks.
I love to hear her speak, yet well I know
That music hath a far more pleasing sound:
I grant I never saw a goddess go,
My mistress, when she walks, treads on the ground:
     And yet, by heaven, I think my love as rare
     As any she belied with false compare.

TIME SUSTAINING TRUTH

(Painted by Nicolas Poussin. Mussée du Louvre.)

SHAKESPEARE
THE TRUE AUTHORSHIP

by

Dr. Douglas Baker
B.A., M.R.C.S., L.R.C.P.

First edition: 1976
This edition: 1994

ISBN 0-906006-90-2

'Little Elephant'
High Road,
Essendon,
Herts,
ENGLAND.

Dedicated to the Memory
of
John Richardson
(A karmic debt repaid)

for
Steven Conger

CONTENTS

AUTHOR'S NOTE

This work makes no attempt to hide the fact that a completely fresh approach has been used to unlock the mysteries surrounding the authorship of the so-called Shakespearean Plays and THE SONNETS. All that is asked of the reader is that new evidence, scanty as it may seem, be given an examination with an open mind. A hundred years ago no one could have dreamed up carbon dating for classifying ancient texts and other objects. Today, uncertain though it's results may sometimes be, carbon dating is accepted almost without argument.

The author, something of an authority on the paranormal for forty years, has used deep meditation to probe events in and around Stratford some 450 years ago. The results were assisted through a karmic link with one of the actual participants in the scenario of that time and place.

This procedure should not seem so strange. More than half the world's population accepts karma as the basis for divine justice and reincarnation as the mechanism by which that justice is achieved.

In North America archaeological searches have been conducted with some success where these have been directed through clairvoyant perception. This should not be surprising when we remember that Henry Schliemann uncovered the remains of Troy through being aware that he had once lived in the area of Troy. The great chemist Kekule acknowledged that he had unravelled the formula for the benzene molecule while in deep reverie.

Schliemann and Kekule used unconventional methods of unfolding the truth. We are entering an era in which meditation, previously restricted to the orient, is becoming part of the westerner's way of life. It is greatly sought after and its effects are physiological as well as psychological, as researchers in many universities have noted. Meditation can produce changes in states of awareness, relaxation of the muscular system and energisation of the central nervous system. Few investigators would deny that meditation allows other means of perception than those obtained through the normal sensory pathways. Are we to rule out such unconventional means of research? Conventional methods up till now have been unfruitful. There is no sign that they will emerge from their backwaters.

The content of The Sonnets, is clearly not fiction. They are the outpouring of a soul at its creative best. They bear testimony to the nature of their author and to those closest to him. If they are read with both academic understanding as well as self-searching sincerity and with all the available historical data in mind, it soon becomes obvious that the author of The Sonnets was not Will Shakespeare.

To make The Sonnets fit into the authorship of Shakespeare you must cut out parts of them that contradict absolutely, Shakespeare's known traits. It would be like the man who based the measurements of a pyramid on a certain theory and then was caught chipping parts of the pyramid away to make the measurements fit!

The subject needs to be approached with sincerity and honesty. If there are lines in The Sonnets that seem to be mumbo-jumbo, we should admit it and not lead each other off into the quagmires of conjecture and pure nonsense. Whole passages fall into this category. Who was the youth? Everyone presumes that it was some rich patron. No wealth alone, or patronage could call forth such soul-searching as we perceive in almost every line of The Sonnets.

Instead we find 'authorities' on the 'Shakespearean' material digging around for patrons, reversing dedication initials to suit their theories, facts distorted and twisted, all to make The Sonnets and The Plays fit the bogus authorship. The 'The Dark Lady'? There is a perfect explanation for the way in which she is described and without having to resort to silly contradictions. Whoever heard of a serious writer of sonnets describing the foul breath of his lover?

No! We need to employ whatever methods are available, so long as they serve to confirm, to check, to add to or deny, the text until the full truth is reached. Personal feelings, preconceived ideas, bias towards heterosexuality or homosexuality, and, in this instance bisexuality, schools of thought, etc., should not enter into it. Investigators should be dispassionate, objective and detached in their search.

The passing years will underline the unique contribution which this book makes to the Shakespearean saga. Patient research into files and records of individuals very close to events and overlooked by current investigators, will confirm many of the statements shedding new light on the subject outlined here. If my readers are completely fair, they will bear in mind that whilst there has been four centuries of research done into the life of Will Shakespeare, research into the life of the true author has hardly begun.

Douglas Baker   England, August 1976.
B.A., M.R.C.S., L.R.C.P.

SHAKESPEARE:

The Bare Facts

SHAKESPEARE:
The Bare Facts

William Shakespeare was born in the typically English market town of Stratford in the county of Warwickshire. The population in that year of 1564 was about two thousand who were either engaged in agriculture or small industry. His father was John Shakespeare, a glove-maker who had married Mary Arden of Wilmcote, a village four miles to the west of Stratford. Their son William was born in April and was christened in the parish church of the Holy Trinity on the 26th April. Three more children followed and our concern here is only with one of them, Joan Shakespeare, William's younger sister.

There is no evidence that William attended the local grammar school but it would seem certain that he did, for education was free for the children of the burgesses of the town. Nearby was the forest of Arden, then much reduced in size and an hour's walk away was the Cotswolds noted for its elegant uplands and the tiny villages built out of grey limestone. This landscape is frequently described in the Shakespearean plays, the forest of Arden being, for instance, the setting for "As You Like It". But it was also the same setting in which the true author of the plays lived in a village barely a league from the heart of Stratford. If there was no record of William Shakespeare attending Stratford Grammar School this was also true for his neighbour who, twelve years his senior, would make Will famous. In fact almost the entire events of childhood which are SUPPOSED, by many authors to have made up the early life of Shakespeare, and the settings in which they occurred, were equally available to this same person, the real author.

Early in the fifteen sixties the first regular English comedies and tragedies were being written in blank verse. They were to set the pattern and tone for the mushroom growth of English theatre for the next four hundred years. In the fifteen seventies the profession of acting, previously regarded as the field of expression for 'sturdy beggars', became legitimised under the patronage of peers of the realm. The first playhouse was built in 1576 in Shoreditch then just north of the city of London. The demand for plays soon became urgent. Will Shakespeare was then twelve years old.

Absolutely nothing is known of the activities of William Shakespeare at school, or immediately after he left school. The 'hidden years' reach into his early twenties. There is only one episode in his life during those years that we know of for sure and it is the very event that brings about a meeting between the boy of eighteen and his benefactor, the true author of the plays, John Richardson. This occurred in November, 1582.

On November 27, William Shakespeare took a licence to marry one Anne Whateley of Temple Grafton, Warwickshire. But Anne Hathaway was already pregnant by Shakespeare. John Richardson had been a close friend of Richard Hathaway, Anne's father who had died recently. He may have been called upon to fill the patriarchal vacancy in an emergency. It may be surmised that, upon hearing of the licence between Shakespeare and the other Anne, John Richardson exercised his duty speedily for on November 28th a special bond was issued. Fulk Sandells and John Richardson, listed as farmers of Stratford, entered a bond exempting the Bishop of Worcester from all liability should any litigation arise from granting William Shakespeare and Anne Hathaway a marriage licence. This was done to expedite their marriage. The bond cost forty pounds, a sizeable sum in those days, almost equal to the sum Shakespeare paid for New Place *(see plate IX)* years later. It is a testament to the high intentions of the two men. This is a noteworthy point. Richardson remained concerned for the Hathaway family even after Anne's marriage to William Shakespeare.

On May 26th 1583 the baptism of William and Anne Shakespeare's daughter Susanna was recorded. For the years between the birth of the couple's twins, Judith and Hamnett on February 2, 1585 and an allusion to Shakespeare by Robert Greene in 1592, documentary evidence concerning Shakespeare's whereabouts and activities is non-existent. Although it has been conjectured that he entered into his father's declining business, became a lawyer, a provincial actor, or a schoolmaster, nothing can be confirmed about this period except that he left his family and went to London where he was established as an actor and a playwright by 1592 when Greene's illuminating attack was hurled against him.

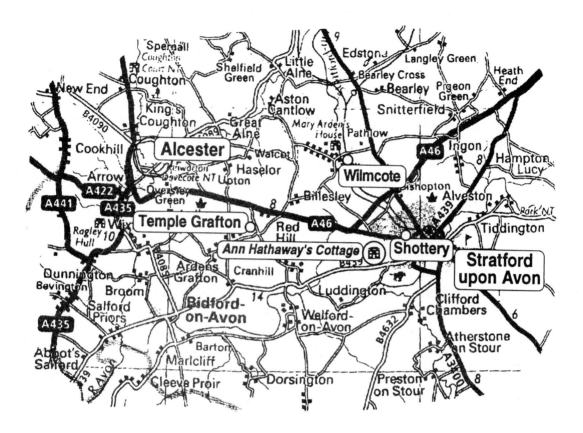

This contemporary map shows Stratford, the site of Shakespeare's birth and also Alcester where the real author was schooled and Temple Grafton where the latter was born. Close to Stratford, is Shottery where many of the events of the two men's lives were enacted. Both grew up in the same environs and were part of the same community. But Shakespeare was twelve years younger and very different in character, profession and religious convictions. Others places on the map, referred to in the text are Snitterfield and Wilmcote.

The dates of publication of VENUS AND ADONIS and THE RAPE OF LUCRECE as April 18, 1593 and May 9, 1594 respectively, are important dates to remember, especially when considering the time period in which the sonnets were written.

Shakespeare did not severe his ties with Stratford, although he did not return to live there permanently until 1610. During this twenty year period, he engaged in numerous business transactions in Stratford, including the purchase of New Place in 1597.

His life in London is equally barren of factual information. We know he was there in 1592 at the time of Robert Greene's attack *(see plate IV)*. His residence is surmised from tax reports of tax collectors which place him in St. Helen's Parish before 1596 and on Bankside in Southwark, near the future Globe Theatre, in 1597. A record of payment from the Master of Revels to the Chamberlain's Men for a performance at court in 1594 lists William Shakespeare as a leading actor and sharer in the company. Yet, how he came to join the Lord Chamberlain's acting company or where he got his training is unknown. Lengthy and imaginative suppositions have been offered, but they cannot be verified.

By 1599, the Chamberlain's Men moved into the new Globe Theatre which was half owned by Richard Burbage, the leading actor of the company, while the remaining shares were equally divided by five actor-sharers, including William Shakespeare. It was a unique ownership arrangement which enabled the actors to retain the bulk of the profits. For Shakespeare it meant he received an income as a dramatist and an actor and profits from the theatre itself. The reputation of the Globe grew until it basked in unrivalled prominence. In the same year, 1599 two of the sonnets, numbers 138 and 144 were included in the collection of verse entitled THE PASSIONATE PILGRIM issued by William Jaggard.

Queen Elizabeth died in 1603. Upon James I's succession to the throne, all acting companies were declared to be under the patronage of members of the Royal Family. The Chamberlain's Men were considered to be the finest troupe in London and soon became the King's Men. For Shakespeare, even greater personal prominence resulted. In 1608, it is known that seven men, including Shakespeare, had shares in a second theatre called Blackfriars, which they rented.

Shakespeare continued to act as late as 1603, well after his fame was established as the playwright and poet. Little reliable evidence exists about the parts he played in his own or other's plays. The most crucial 'black hole' in information for our case here regards the 'when and how' of Shakespeare's purported dramatic writing. He offered the plays for use and for publication but beyond this, nothing is known of how the plays came to be written or of the circumstances of their extensive output.

Shakespeare's will was very ordinary except for two factors, one of which seems to have been overlooked by investigators. Shakespeare made no mention of the plays being 'his' plays in the will at all. It is true that legally, these belonged to the King's Men and to the publishers but, at the same time, one would have expected some comment on them in so lengthy a document as the will was and considering that they were the main source of the wealth being disposed of by the will.

The lesser noted factor is that he seems to have been extraordinarily generous to his sister Joan in leaving the house in Henley Street to her at a nominal rent of 12 pence per annum for the rest of her life. She was married with three children and had a hatter's business.

THE TRUE AUTHOR

THE TRUE AUTHOR

A few miles to the west of Stratford is the tiny village of Temple Grafton through which there runs a brook, once called Temple Brook. In a small hamlet on the Temple Brook Estate, John Richardson was born very early in the 1550's, probably in 1552. He was of humble parents and records of them and his early life do not seem to exist. He seems to have had some formal education but, as with Shakespeare, we have no record of it.

He was a restless boy with such a love of nature and tender things that he would usually be first to rise in the household, not only to help with the farm chores, but to visit those precious animals which had won his special affection and, with equal concern, to observe the progress of plants that he had himself sown. He was fascinated by the spectacle of dawn and drank up the mythology related to it:-

> Full many a glorious morning have I seen
> Flatter the mountain-tops with sovereign eye....

And then again:-

> Hark, hark! the lark at Heaven's gate sings,
>   And Phoebus 'gins arise,
> His steeds to water at those springs
>   On chaliced flowers that lies;
> And winking Mary-buds begin
>   To ope their golden eyes:
> With everything that pretty is,
>   My lady sweet, arise:
>   Arise, arise.

John attended the school in Alcester, three miles away. It was cramped and unappealing to a boy who loved to be out with nature. The schooling was rigid, dull and oppressive.

As soon as he was able, he rode on horseback the few miles to school and indeed, spent much of his time in stables and with horses. Until then it was certainly a matter of 'creeping like snail unwillingly to school...'

Later, in his plays, he was to voice some of his detestation for the long hours of scholarly incarceration:-

> I'm no breeching scholar in the schools
> I'll not be tied to hours, nor pointed times.

His own teacher was nature:-

> And this our life, exempt from public haunt,
> Finds tongues in trees, books in the running brooks,
> Sermons in stones, and good in everything:
> I would not change it.

But at school John Richardson did read Ovid in the original, as well as in translation, as any schoolboy of the time would have. The sources of Venus and Adonis, are found in Books IV and X of Ovid's Metamorphoses. Lucrece blends such classical sources as Ovid, Livy and Virgil.

An education in history in Elizabethan times re-emphasised the classical with such standard texts as Caesar's 'Gallic Wars', Sallust's 'Jugurthine Wars' and Livy's 'History of Rome'.

It is apparent from the works themselves that Richardson favoured Ovid, Terence, Plautus, Seneca, Roman history, as well as the entire panorama of English history. Richardson was an avid reader, able to work on his own, away from school and later read Greek and Latin.It is probable that Johnson's poor opinion of the works Latin and Greek was based on his personal conversations with Shakespeare. It was certainly not based on the 'Shakespearean' plays which Richardson wrote. They showed scholarship in Latin if not in Greek.

We have noted that life in the saddle began very young for John Richardson. So expert a horseman did he become that by the time he was sixteen, he was already able to ride as a courier. During the sixteenth century, there were many for whom the carrying of private letters and packages became a livelihood. It was called the 'Stranger's Post' and letters travelling by this method covered ground at an average of six or seven miles an hour, fine weather or foul. Stratford was not only on a main road from London to the north but was the hub of many roads that radiated outwards to important places like Worcester, Gloucester, Oxford and Banbury. The provision of horses in fresh relays, and of couriers too, was important work and the youth, with his love of riding, soon got caught up in it. He found that contracting for furniture removals was lucrative and his powerful physique responded to the challenge.

In his writings later, he demonstrated his special knowledge of horses. The countryside that his employment took him into also featured in his plays. He himself rode great distances, invariably spending the night at wayside inns. Innkeepers acted as postmasters in those days, caring for parcels and dispatches to be collected by couriers. In this work young John met every conceivable kind of character which made up a cross-section of the nation. These encounters were to assist him in casting the characters for his plays. And so the long hours spent in the evening at hostelries and inns were not entirely wasted. There he met other couriers and exchanged with them the current news and stories from all over the kingdom. Often his work took him as far as Bristol where he met sea-faring men, or even up to London. He passed Berkeley Castle many times and later mentioned it in his plays. Hard work was his constant companion, whether at home or on the road:-

> Weary with toil, I haste me to my bed,
> The dear repose for limbs with travel tired;
> But then begins a journey in my head,
> To work my mind, when body's works expired:
> For then my thoughts, from far where I abide,
> Intend a zealous pilgrimage to thee,
> And keep my drooping eyelids open wide,
> Looking on darkness which the blind do see:
> Save that my soul's imaginary sight
> Presents thy shadow to my sightless view,
> Which like a jewel hung in the ghastly night,
> Makes black night beauteous and her old face new.
>   Lo, thus, by day my limbs, by night my mind,
>   For thee and for myself no quiet find.

Sonnet 27

Anyone who has ridden horseback hard all day, or has sailed a boat for many hours anchored to the helm, will understand the meaning of the first four lines. They describe an appearance common to men who travel great distances with a motion that constantly repeats itself so that when the body is exhausted the brain, really the mind, remains active. In this sonnet, the out-of-body experience (which science now calls 'lucid dreaming') is described. It is often associated with daylong travel.

Those that doubt that the true author was an expert horseman, when Shakespeare himself surely was not, should read The Sonnets again and then glance too into VENUS AND ADONIS. These excursions would soon correct their misapprehension:-

> How heavy do I journey on the way,
> When what I seek, my weary travels' end,
> Doth teach that ease and that repose to say,
> 'Thus far the miles are measured from thy friend!'
> The beast that bears me, tired with my woe,
> Plods dully on, to bear that weight in me,
> As if by some instinct the wretch did know
> His rider loved not speed, being made from thee:
> The bloody spur cannot provoke him on
> That sometimes anger thrusts into his hide;
> Which heavily he answers with a groan,
> More sharp to me than spurring to his side;
> > For that same groan doth put this to my mind;
> > My grief lies onward, and my joy behind.

Sonnet 50

The sonnet describes the rider, depressed at leaving his beloved, tired and disconsolate and conveying to the animal his sentiments. In VENUS AND ADONIS there is a different mood:-

> So did this horse excel a common one,
> In shape, in courage, colour, pace and bone.

Round-hoof'd, short-jointed, fetlocks shag and long,
Broad breast, full eye, small head, and nostrils wide,
High crest, short ears, straight legs and passing strong,
Thin mane, thick tail, broad buttock, tender hide:
    Look, what a horse should have he did not lack,
    Save a proud rider on so proud a back.

Sometimes he scuds far off, and there he stares;
Anon he starts at stirring of a feather;
To bid the wind a base he now prepares,
And whe'r he run or fly they know not whether:
    For through his mane and tail the high wind sings,
    Fanning the hairs, who wave like feather'd wings.

These are the words of a man who understands horses, who has ridden them, who has bought and sold them. I have emphasised this factor in John Richardson's life for reasons which will emerge later.

His adolescence was marked by an inordinate urge for freedom, and later, this grew into a healthy respect for self-independence:-

Such wind as scatters young men through the world
To seek their fortunes further than at home
Where small experience grows.

He liked to have many irons in the fire and learned to keep all of them at white heat. In his early years, real joy came to him through his contact with the many people that those irons reached. He was fascinated with them and by their problems, conflicts and reactions.

The carrying of furniture and chattels all over Warwickshire by waggon brought him into the homes and the lives of persons in every walk of life. Their behaviour, poor, rich or famous, was the ground substance of his works. It was hard work and it was to mature him very rapidly. It lined his face and chopped his features, as the sonnets show:-

But when my glass shows me myself indeed,
Beated and chopp'd with tanned antiquity.....

29

He soon put his journeys to better use and merely contracted out the removal work. His visits to the big cities encouraged him into trading. The small refinements which women look to and which were offered more readily in London, he transported in his emptied waggons into the provinces, to Warwickshire and even beyond. He knew what people wanted and catered for their special needs. He was never to lose that deep understanding of how people thought and wished and of their psychological needs and he catered for them in the plays. The latest in pharmaceuticals and cosmetics were always on demand and easily transported. He could put a package together to win any buyer. The art was later extended into the format of his plays. Scenes, acts and even whole plays were packaged with adequate comic relief as well as the everyday matter of tragedy and contemporary history.

Richardson met every kind of rogue and learned quickly to discover an underlying story or news event. He loved gambling and made money from it. No wonder he was so unlucky in love! He shifted his focus to Shottery just near Stratford where he bought a farm freehold. It was somewhere for his business and somewhere he could settle for there was a new urge in his young mind. He wanted to write down the many incidents in his life and was caught up in the sudden emergence of the Elizabethan theatre. Shottery was where his cartage horses and those faster animals used in the work of couriering could be rested and re-equipped and where his merchandise could be stored. More than anything, Shottery was a place where he could bring his friends, where he could rest and where he could spend the long winter nights in writing.

A rough diamond, cut and hewed by the vicissitudes imposed on a spiritual and sensitive person born into humble circumstances, he had, nevertheless, a great tenderness which he displayed when confronted with friends and acquaintances. He could develop a rapport with anyone he chose, man, woman or child, instantly. It was to provide him with the hundreds of characters in the plays.

He could sweep aside differences in intellect, disparities in physique, income and social standing in a moment and then find some point of common interest on which to build a relationship which could be taken to the ultimate, a casting of the character in some part of his works. In this and in other respects, he was a manipulator and a user. His associations often took on the nature of a whirlwind. Almost before the rapport was established, he was gone, on his way like a will-of-the-wisp, leaving his companions a little bewildered, but never with unpleasant memories. The young Shakespeare was to discover just this lightning tendency when Richardson dramatically intervened in his courtship and changed his way of life for all time.

Richardson was a master of confrontation. A bumptious official, a surly innkeeper, an incompetent groom, they would all feel the whip of his tongue which was no less effective than his quill, if they attracted his attention.

He would choose the time and the place, and even the correct vernacular, to administer a mental or verbal whipping that would be remembered by the recipient, as well as onlookers for many a day. We suspect that sometimes, if the personality interested him enough, he would want to see it at its best and at its worst. This comes out no better demonstrated than in the third part of Henry VI, when the Duke of York, about to be murdered, turns on his murderess, the Queen Margaret, and spits out invective that must have taken the audience by storm. It certainly impressed and enraged Robert Greene whose significant comments are dealt with later. It was hardly what one would have expected from the 'gentle Shakespeare' who was so even tempered that he could never play anything but the smallest parts:-

> She-wolf of France, but worse than wolves of France,
> Whose tongue more poisons than the adder's tooth!
> How ill-beseeming is it in thy sex
> To triumph like an Amazonian trull
> Upon their woes whom fortune captivates!
> But that thy face is visard-like, unchanging,
> Made impudent with evil deeds,
> I would assay, proud queen, to make thee blush:
> To tell thee whence thou cam'st, of whom deriv'd,
> Were shame enough to shame thee, wert thou not shameless.
> Thy father bears the title King of Naples,
> Of both the Sicils and Jerusalem,
> Yet not so wealthy as an English yeoman.
> Hath that poor monarch taught thee to insult?

> 'Tis beauty that doth oft make women proud;
> But, God He knows, thy share thereof is small.
> 'Tis virtue that doth make them most admir'd;
> The contrary doth make thee wonder'd at.
> 'Tis government that makes them seem divine;
> The want thereof makes thee abominable
> Thou art as opposite to every good
> As the Antipodes are unto us,
> Or as the south to the septentrion.
> O tiger's heart wrapped in a woman's hide!

Shakespeare was no Plates tiger but Richardson could be and frequently was when action or confrontation was demanded. Enemies he made, here and there, but never through being unfair. He was a just man and valued justice. He wrote a whole play, THE MERCHANT OF VENICE on that theme. His enemies came as the result of his intolerance of pettiness, offhandedness, intolerance and injustice:-

> For who would bear the whips and scorns of time,
> The oppressor's wrong, the proud man's contumely,
> The pangs of dispriz'd love, the law's delay,
> The insolence of office.....

The processes of law feature frequently in the plots he used and in major or minor themes, as, for instance, in the graveyard scene in HAMLET.

There are those who even say that the author whoever he was must have spent some time as a clerk to an attorney. It is far more likely that Richardson gained his legal knowledge from sporting with the lads of the Inns of Court in his younger days on visits to London.

LUTHER AT THE DIET OF WORMS

(From the picture by Delpérèe.)

He disliked matters religious except where they reached to the highest authority. The pope was not regarded as high enough. The sentiments of Paracelsus (1493-1541) were appealing to him, that Martin Luther and the Pope were like two whores arguing over their chastity. Yet he was capable of intense religious feeling when stirred by nature or beauty in Man:-

> How many a holy and obsequious tear
> Hath dear religious love stol'n from my eye....

Richardson was no atheist and detested expressions of it in Marlowe, whom he met later. But then he was also no Catholic sympathiser or recusant where as there is good evidence that the Shakespeare family not only stemmed directly from Catholic forebears but maintained their sentiments secretly and sometimes even openly. Shakespeare's father was censored for not attending the Protestant church in Stratford. John Richardson regarded the clergy of both sides as humbugs. He never attended church and was far too mobile to fall under the not too strict disciplines of the Baudy Courts for this offence. In two plays he railed against papists:-

> What earthly name to interrogatories
> Can task the free breath of a sacred king?
> Thou canst not, cardinal, devise a name
> So slight, unworthy, and ridiculous,
> To charge me to answer, as the Pope.
> Tell him this tale; and from the mouth of England
> Add thus much more, - that no Italian priest
> Shall tithe or toll in our dominions;

Hardly words expected from a dramatist with a family background of Catholic sympathies! Richardson subscribed to the belief in The Divine Right of Kings current at that time and later to bring about the doom of the Stuart monarchy. The speech quoted above from KING JOHN goes on:-

> But as we, under heaven, are supreme head,
> So, under him, that great supremacy,
> Where we do reign, we will alone uphold,
> Without th'assistance of a mortal hand:
> So tell the pope; all reverence set apart
> To him and his usurp'd authority.

Bernard Shaw even commented on the fact that despite Shakespeare deriving from a Catholic family, his plays contain no figures that are Catholic. Rather, they are all intensely Protestant. Richardson's family were intensely Protestant and remained so long after his death. John Richardson's eldest son, also John, born 1578, was church warden in 1636 at Shottery, a confirmed Protestant.

A Century later, Parson Richard Davies said that Shakespeare died a papist and certainly, even in Stratford today, there are many who would not disagree too violently. But John Richardson respected order. His journeys had brought him quickly to realise that the miseries of England had been brought by bad government and through the barons who had threatened the monarchy. A weak monarchy spelt difficulties all the way down to the common man with whom he had such sympathy. The robber barons, the petty officials, corrupt, decadent and obsequious goaded him to fury, a fury that was often reflected in his plays.

In his early life John Richardson had many loves, as we shall soon note, but among those that dominated his life was the love of theatre. He travelled widely and made sure that if he could possibly arrange it, his path would cross that of a company of players. Strange urges overtook him after a performance, urges to create something similar, or rather, to create something that would provide the same sentiments as flooded him when the final act of the plays he watched concluded.

Relationships that extended beyond the first brief encounter, lasted because he wanted them to. His sincerity was deep and his capacity to love could show in many ways. He served the interests of his friends and promoted their well-being whenever he could. Affection to him had, in many instances, to lead on to something more intimate and the nature of his fluidic existence, always on the move, sought impatiently for immediate response before he travelled on.

Oft-times his companions were from the theatre in whose company he felt most relaxed. It was usually male company and always included boy actors which was the norm in periods when drama was of a high quality.

John Richardson emerged from these relationships bi-sexual, accepting that a pretty face or handsome figure that could be coaxed into response was an invitation to share beauty. The sharing brought him an elevation of both consciousness and vitality that made him creative at other levels. It showed again and again in his poetry and verse that began to pour from him. VENUS AND ADONIS was not an elaborate attempt primarily to obtain a patron. That was Shakespeare's idea later formulated. The poem was the natural outcome of his elevated feelings during the relationships of this period. The poem suggests an equal love for both sexual types depicted in it.

Richardson's enthusiasm for beauty knew no barriers. He took risks and provoked scandal and yet was always reticent about his genius. Most genuine artists, inspired by the muses are not anxious to assume the role of the one and only originator of their works. It was not difficult, when the time came, for Richardson to remain in the shadows, reticent about his genius, hidden deliberately from the world and it was only after his death that someone who loved him stepped forward to put matters right. Only later, when death was but a few years off did he sense his immortality and his genius and he stated it clearly in The Sonnets. There was something else, far more important than public acclaim which John sought. It was in the realm of love rather than that of the arts, if these can be separated from each other at all.

Beauty of form, whether in nature or in man was a challenge to him. He had to rise to it. Recording it was one way, sharing it at its own level was the other way. Only when he settled at Shottery could he begin to record rather than to share. The harsh pace of life slowed; experiences need no longer become just memories. Once written down exactly as they occurred or were related to him, they no longer itched in his brain. Sometimes they called forth instant poetic form, sometimes they were framed rapidly into the most magnificent prose. Initially, there was no attempt to force the fragments into completed poems or even into the plays. That all began to come later.

That beauty is the prerogative of one sex he dispelled in VENUS AND ADONIS.

The opening speech of Venus hails Adonis as more beautiful than her own fair features:-

> 'Thrice fairer than myself,' thus she began,
> 'The field's chief flower, sweet above compare,
> Stain to all nymphs, more lovely than a man,
> More white and red than doves or roses are;
> Nature that made thee, with herself at strife,
> Saith that the world hath ending with thy life.'

And, more intimately, the same poem describes the boy:-

> Once more the ruby-colour'd portal opened
> Which to his speech did honey passage yield;
> Like a red morn, that ever betoken'd
> Wreck to the seamen, tempest to the field'
> Sorrow to shepherds, woe unto the birds....

*   *   *   *   *   *

The house at Shottery was large and unmanageable. It required the female touch. In any case Richardson wanted to settle down to writing. There is no record so far of when he married but his first child, a girl, was baptised Rose on the 20 May 1574. This marriage, the first of two, was, from his point of view, not a happy one but it grumbled along. More children were born :-

Joan, 30 November 1575
John, 15 July 1578
William, 24 April 1581

The marriage ended with the death of his wife in childbirth. The problems of house-keeping were now aggravated further by the presence of young children. Richard had a close friend in Shottery, his neighbour Fulk Sandells who was about ten years his junior. They were good companions and travelled frequently by horse together. It was Sandells who accompanied Richardson on the memorable ride to Worcester and helped him to bring pressure to bear on William Shakespeare to do the right thing by his neighbour's daughter Anne Hathaway. Richardson had many opportunities

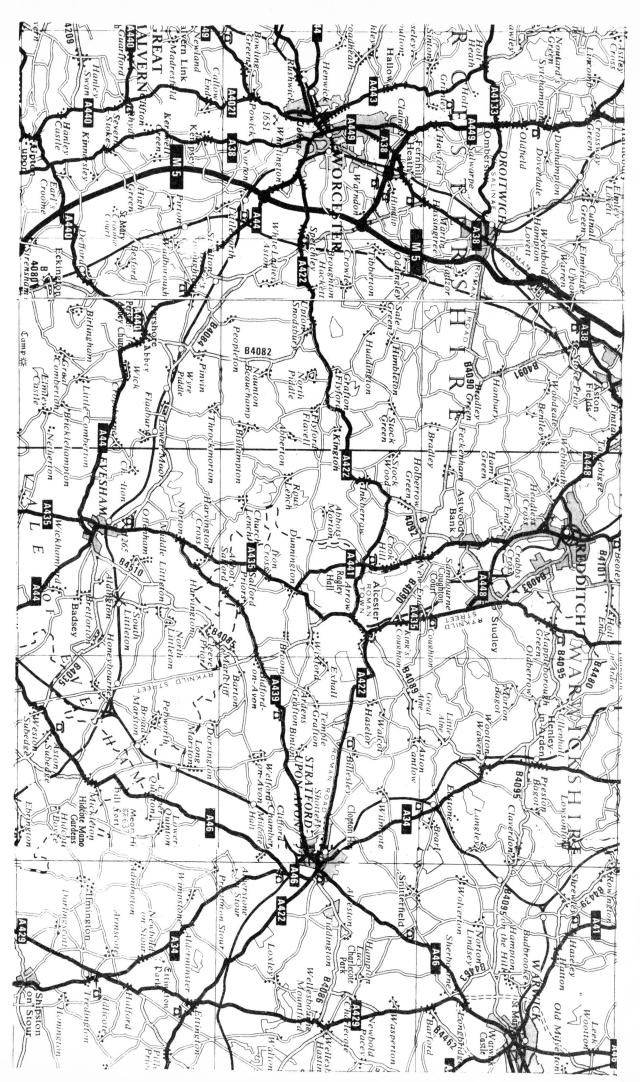

Richardson and Sandells rode from Shottery to Worcester to stand surety for the marriage of William Shakespeare to Anne Hathaway.

(Possible routes are shown in this contemporary map.)

to observe Fulk's sister Mary Sandells, a quiet, unemotional girl with a propensity for minding her own business. She never remarked the closeness of friendship between her brother and Richardson and the latter chose her for his second wife, and the mother to his three children. This second marriage was a success considering the many problems that faced it. Richardson had matured and the humane psychology conspicuous in his plays was beginning to operate domestically. It is a tribute to Mary that he wrote at least one of his sonnets on his relationship with her, in which both, with eyes to see, did not look too hard at each other:

> When my love swears that she is made to truth,
> I do believe her, though I know she lies,
> That she might think me some untutor'd youth,
> Unlearned in the world's false subtleties.
> Thus vainly thinking that she thinks me young,
> Although she knows my days are past the best,
> Simply I credit her false-speaking tongue:
> On both sides thus is simple truth suppress'd.
> But wherefore says she not she is unjust?
> And wherefore say not I that I am old?
> O, love's best habit is in seeming trust,
> And age in love loves not to have years told.
> > Therefore I lie with her and she with me,
> > And in our faults by lies we flatter'd be.

Sonnet 138

These are surely the words of a man more likely to be in his early forties than in his late twenties as was Shakespeare at this time.

Four children, Mary, Fulk, John and Margaret were born between the years 1583 and 1592, indicating that the marriage worked despite the extreme pressures on John Richardson.

Richardson's other neighbour of long standing in Shottery was Richard Hathaway. He lived, with his large family at Hewland Farm now known as Anne Hathaway's Cottage, and Anne was his eldest daughter by his first wife. His second marriage had produced three boys. In 1581 Hathaway died.

John Richardson had been a signatory to his will and, besides this, a good friend. It behoved him to be of assistance to the family in their hour of need. That came sooner than he expected. Anne, a woman of twenty-six, fell pregnant to a young caller by the name of Will Shakespeare who was eighteen. He was not impressed with the boy, who appeared to be something of a lay-about, and was sure that Anne could manage her young lover in her own way. However, matters suddenly took on a serious note. He was a native of Temple Grafton and knew the villagers well. Word came to him with deft speed that William had also been courting a girl in that village by the name of Ann Whateley, a girl of his own age. The word was that the two were to be wed. The proof was that a marriage licence had been issued and it was not recorded in the Worcester episcopal register.

Richardson, a man of action and a master at confrontation, went to work immediately. With his close friend Fulk Sandells, later his brother-in-law, he confronted William. The outcome was that the youth agreed to do the right thing by Anne Hathaway. Richardson had to act fast. The day after the licence was issued to bring Will and Anne Whateley into wedlock, he and Fulk Sandells rode to Worcester and stood surety for the issuing of a second licence for the marriage of William Shakespeare to Anne Hathaway. This meant that Richardson and Sandells agreed to pay forty pounds if any legal matter arose to prevent the marriage. The bishop of Worcester and his officials were thus indemnified against any suit or action which might develop from this entry. Now, instead of a delay due to the reading of the banns three times, only a single reading was necessary. The effect was that the marriage could take place earlier and when Shakespeare's daughter was born the couple had been married six months.

We have already noted that the sum of forty pounds was remarkable. Richardson, when he died only left, with his other effects, a cash sum of seventy pounds in his will. It does show the extent to which Richardson held in esteem the family matters of the Hathaways. It should be remembered that Anne was Shakespeare's wife for many years and outlived him. It is unlikely that she would have disregarded such an act of goodwill on the part of Richardson. It is also unlikely that she, being so close to Richardson, would not *** known that he was the author of the plays. Such knowledge, even after the passage of many years, could be held as a warning to her husband to play the game, financially, with regard to her side of the family which would include the Richardsons and with regard to his own fidelity.

Two important factors emerge from this event. The character of Richardson shows a man of powerful stature, capable of intervening, manipulating and concluding in matters of great significance to the lives of others. It also shows that Shakespeare was susceptible to his influence and that he must have played the part of a junior member in a family that embraced the Hathaways, the Richardsons and the Sandells. If he could be made to toe the line once, with regard to Anne Hathaway, he could be made to do it again. He was, in his younger days, ill-equipped to do aught else. Later, the Richardsons married into the Hathaway family and, as we have already noted, Mary Sandells became John Richardson's second wife. Whether Shakespeare ever forgave the interference with his marital affairs, we don't know. It does seem that he trod very warily of his wife and her connections or loyalties. In the purchasing of property in London later, he made sure that, in the event of his death, it would not get into his wife's hands. His own loyalties moved towards a different section of the family. His sister Joan and, later, his daughter and her husband, Dr. Hall, became the focus for his attentions. We shall see that he was only able to solve this matter effectively well after the death of Richardson.

Despite everything, the Richardson family became quite gregarious. The house at Shottery became a focal point for the families mentioned and as Richardson now gave more and more of his time to writing, events which developed later virtually anchored him to Shottery and gave him the time to produce that massive output of plays and poems that has astounded all ages and in a period half as long as previously assessed! He wrote day and night in the great living room of the house, reclining on his left side on a couch there. He wrote on several themes simultaneously. The manuscripts were placed in a huge wine barrel in the dining room. From there, they could be extracted and worked on without difficulty.

At first, Richardson had no idea that he was possessed of genius. There were no standards by which to measure the quality of his dramatic writing. "Genius, for what?" might well have been asked. He had assembled a vast amount of material, much of it from certain well-known books, had put much of it into verse, woven a plot or two. He had written a deal of poetry which lacked style and form. It did not seem to have much point to it. But the urge was there; it was an overwhelming desire to bring to life his own version of the vivid events of the histories. He set them down in what were to become the Chronicle Plays. Visitors, family and friends helped sort out the accumulated mass of material.

One of these was William Shakespeare now in his mid-twenties. He had always been welcome at the Richardson's home. In the late 1580's, restless and unsettled, Will had drifted to London. He had an interest in theatre mainly through Richardson, whom he knew to be working on plays. In London, he had been fitfully employed in various menial tasks with numerous groups of players. Even so, as a hireling, he had accumulated, and brought back to Stratford some very useful experience Richardson was to find extremely helpful.

When the plague struck London and the theatre closed, Will went back to Stratford. He now became a frequent visitor at Shottery. Far into the night he would listen to Richardson reading over his plays, his poems, and, sometimes, but rarely, the sonnets. He commented and advised on the dramatic appeal which the manuscripts would make to the groups of players and their audiences in London. Before then, Richardson had delivered a few manuscripts himself to the players for performance. Amongst these was Titus Andronicus. It was no gentle play and there has always been comment about whether the "gentle" Shakespeare could have written it.

Well, he didn't. Richardson did, and he delivered it. The first author to attribute the play to someone else than Shakespeare was Edward Ravenscroft. He wrote:

> "I have been told by some ancient conversant with the stage
> that it was not originally his, but brought by a private author
> to be acted and he (Shakespeare) only gave some master-
> touches to one or two of the principal parts or characters."*

Ravenscroft cites no authority for this story; yet most 18th-century scholars, including Lewis Theobald and Dr. Johnson, held this view.*

*A Shakespeare Encyclopaedia, page 880 Met Authorhuen & Co.

Thereafter, the next few plays were delivered to the players by Shakespeare until a different arrangement was made, and which will be discussed later. The function of Shakespeare, at this stage, in the early nineties, was to ensure that the plays reached the actors for acting and not the publishers. In those days, when no copyright laws existed, it was difficult to stop the pirating of dramatic material. Despite precautions, actor's manuscripts were copied and unscrupulous publishers put them into print. Players in the provinces thus obtained the plays and paid nothing to the playwright for performing them. Shakespeare had had experience already with altering, adding to, and subtracting from available materials and formulating the results into a single play. In this way, mainly with the help of Richardson's material, he was able to put together the play Henry VI, in three parts. Shakespeare, returning to Stratford, urged Richardson to give him more plays. The financial returns were hardly rewarding but the plays were doing well. It was through Shakespeare showing some of Richardson's manuscripts to the Lord Chamberlain's company that he was invited to join them, an offer which he accepted with alacrity.

In the early nineties, no one seemed very concerned as to who had written the play and there was no point in emphasising authorship. No doubt, as Richardson's output increased, he would have begun to insist on his name being used, and even perhaps he would have moved to London to the scene of things, as Shakespeare himself had suggested but in the late eighties an event had occurred that altered everything and mainly in Shakespeare's favour. Richardson met W.H.

Richardson's handwriting was atrocious and for this reason alone it would have been necessary to have all manuscripts copied out. He wrote incessantly whenever he was not with W.H., allowing no discomfort or circumstances to halt him entirely. When racked with rheumatism, he sprawled on the couch in the living room with parchment spread on a low table so that his right hand could race freely tracing out unrestrictedly the prose or verse. He was constantly jotting notes down with any lines of verse that might nudge their way into his attention. As he clattered into the courtyard of an inn, doing work he could not avoid, even before the ostler had led the horse away, he would call for quills.

VENVS
AND ADONIS

Vilia miretur vulgus: mihi flauus Apollo
Pocula Castalia plena ministret aqua.

LONDON

Imprinted by Richard Field, and are to be sold at
the signe of the white Greyhound in
Paules Church-yard.
1593.

VENUS AND ADONIS was the first work to be published.

He was never didactic in his writing, pressing home some point beyond the limit of its interest. He would never set out meticulously to create a scene or act which accurately described the medieval scene of his day, or of the country of the play's particular setting. He would, instead, assemble in his mind all the elements of the scene, the historic background, the atmosphere, the conflicts, major and minor, and the characters and he would place himself amongst it all as if he were the principal participant. Frequently, he would develop preferences for roles that he had created, discarding those that interested him lease. Whenever he could, he used real life situations drawn from his vast reservoir of personal experiences. Venus and Adonis was written in this way with W.H. in the role of Adonis.

His pastoral works were drawn from direct observation whenever possible. Even Lucrece was written through his having himself ranged through the whole gamut of passion that it portrays. The labouring breath of grief or that of mounting ecstasy speak the same language and he found no human instinct or behaviour without its describable counterpart in nature. The arches of a bridge, like the teeth, allow the surging forces, peculiar to their setting to pass through them, to and fro:

> But wretched as he is, he strives in vain;
> What he breathes out his breathe drinks up again.
> As through an arch the violent roaring tide
> Outruns the eye that doth behold his haste,
> Yet in the eddy boundeth in, his pride
> Back to the strait that forc'd him on so fast;
> In rage sent out, recall'd in rage, being past;
> Even so his sighs, his sorrows, make a saw,
> To push grief on, and back the same grief draw.

He never saw the behaviour of men as opposed to or separate from nature, the supreme mother to all things.

He himself had tasted the agony and the ecstasy of all passionate experiences:

> The expense of spirit in a waste of shame
> Is lust in action; and till action, lust
> Is perjured, murderous, bloody, full of blame,
> Savage, extreme, rude, cruel, not to trust;
> Enjoy'd no sooner but despised straight;
> Past reason hunted; and no sooner had,
> Past reason hated, a swallowed bait,
> On purpose laid to make the taker mad:
> Mad in pursuit, and in possession so;
> Had, having, and in quest to have, extreme;
> A bliss in proof, and proved, a very woe;
> Before, a joy proposed; behind, a dream.
> All this world well knows; yet none knows well
> To shun the heaven that leads men to this hell.

It is tempting to see this experience as a sexual one. In fact it is written during alcoholic remorse, a remorse not made easier to W.H.'s own aversion to such occurrences, even though they were rare.

On one of his travels to Oxford, Richardson met Robert Greene,* six years his junior, a brilliant young man fresh from both Oxford and Cambridge universities, with Master's degrees in Art. The acquaintance was renewed again later when Greene, after a disastrous marriage, moved to London. He was a handsome man and very much at the heart of theatrical affairs in the Captial City. He had travelled to France and Italy and was filled with remarkable ideas and enthusiasm. He worked hard and played hard and in matters sexual, was not all that discriminating.

---

*Greene, Robert (c. 1558-92). Poet, playwright and pamphleteer. Born at Norwich, Green was educated at Cambridge, where he received his Master of Arts degree in 1588. Five years later he received a degree from Oxford, and made a point of parading his academic titles in some of his published works. Some time before this he travelled in France and Italy, drawn thither, if we are to believe him, by the persuasions of the 'lewd wags' who were his university friends, such as Nashe and Peel. He married in 1585, but soon left his wife for London and a life of resolute dissipation prodigious even by the impressive standards of his day.

Richardson** found him entertaining and useful. A little money spent on Greene, a meal reinforced with flagon of rhenish (which Richardson would not touch if he could help it) and there were long nights back in his lodgings in which Richardson could be brought up to date with the London scene and they could read each other's new works. Greene told about his travels in Europe and persuaded Richardson to set some of his plays in Italian and French settings. It was from this source that Richardson obtained part of the material for Henry VI, referred to later. The matter of Richardson using Shakespeare as a "front", a device which Greene disapproved of, was also raised.

Robert Greene is often quoted as an example of a literary man who set out, at the very beginning to supply what his public wanted. He was prolific and wrote some thirty-five works in twelve years. It was from Greene that Richardson also 'purchased' a lyric for use in his play The Winter's Tale. When, later, Shakespeare was being credited with authorship of the play, Greene was livid.

** A COMEDY OF ERRORS is acknowledged to be one of the earliest of the plays. John Richardson's association with Robert Greene injected much of the linga franca of that time. In this work there appears the phrase 'Something in the wind' which dates from 1571. This points to the possibility that Richardson was writing his earliest works from 1575 when he was about 23 and Shakespeare 11 or 12 years old.

He was a prolific writer, beginning with imitations of the Euphuistic mode made fashionable by Lyly and going on from there to produce pastoral romances modelled on Sidney's Arcadia. Of these, Pandosto (1585) is notable not only for the charming lyrics scattered throughout it, but also because it was the direct source of Shakespeare's The Winter's Tale in the 1590's. Greene, by his own account, abandoned Chaucer for the more moral Gower and produced a series of serious didactic works such as Greene's Vision (written 1590, published posthumously). In many of these the moral purpose is purely formal. His plays include Alphonsus, King of Aragon (1588), an ill-advised attempt to match Marlowe's mighty line; an attack on contemporary corruption. A Looking Glass for London and England (c. 1590), written in collaboration with Thomas Lodge; and Friar Bacon and Friar Bungay (c. 1591), his best play, a romantic comedy which handles the necromantic theme of Dr.Faustus rather more lightly than Marlowe.

But Greene's intrinsic interest as a literary figure rests on the most explicitly autobiographical of his writings. These can be roughly divided into those in which Greene casts himself in the role of an abjectly penitent sinner confessing his evil deeds and those in which he gives a more detached account of some of the activities of the London underworld he knew so well. To the first group belongs Greene's Groatsworth of Wit (published posthumously in 1592), in which he repents, among other things, of the evil example afforded by the lives of his former friends, Marlowe, Nashe and Peele. (From British & Commonwealth Literature, edited by David Daiches, Penguin Books.)

Greene, for all his dissolute ways, fired Richardson with his same desire to write seriously. THE WINTER'S TALE was not John Richardson's first play. He had already put together three others;-

THE TAMING OF THE SHREW
THE COMEDY OF ERRORS
TWO GENTLEMEN OF VERONA.

They all pre-dated 1589 and several good authorities support this contention. It is inconceivable that, at the age of twenty-three, Shakespeare could have shown such maturity of style and sophistication. Richardson was, on the other hand, and by now thirty-five, in his second marriage and the father of many children. He had been engaged in writing the CHRONICLE PLAYS.

The output of dramatic material by Richardson was prodigious we know, assuming he was the real author. But the rapidity of his creation is magnified even further when placed amidst the true facts. Almost everything John Richardson wrote was telescoped between 1580 and 1594 and of these fourteen years, the last six years were, by far, the most productive, representing nearly everything after the History Plays.

He was not concerned with meeting deadlines, as one might have expected with such a massive output. He wrote almost nothing to order and was always engaged in several projects at once. From 1590, by which time he had met W.H., the sonnets were being written. They served, with W.H., as a spiritual impetus for all the other dramatic works after that date. There is hardly any comedy or tragedy that does not bear the stamp of being written whilst the sonnets were unfolding. This is the explanation for the fruitfulness of those last years; the maturing pen, the polish, the depth and the height of feeling imparted were totaly inspired by the presence of W.H.

The re-arrangement of his life imposed upon him by the circumstances of his all-consuming fascination for W.H., gave him not only the time to pursue his amour but also that time he needed for his writing. He had been used to long journeys, restlessness, business matters, lack of direction, dissipation of energies.

Meeting the boy, William Hart, changed all that. Every hour was bearable only so long as it was either with the boy or being put to writing, which itself fascinated W.H. The massive floodgates that had held back the surges of Richardson's soul's intent were down. The ultimate confrontation was upon him, and he, the master of confrontation, was ready for it. A boy, fast growing into a youth of breath-taking beauty, was before him, unique in every way, but most unique in being suffused with a spirituality that confounded Richardson, for all his experience.

The soul of W.H. rushed out to meet John and it gilded everything about him. The boy's radiance was the same that stared at him from every flower, every living thing:-

> "Earth's crammed with heaven
> And every common bush afire with God"

as Robert Browning puts it. Or, as the esotericists would have it:-

> The anima mundi, heavenly dew
> Staring from every eye, glowing from every hue.*

Or, as Richardson himself observed:-

> Gilding the object whereupon it gazeth;
> A man in hue, all 'hues' in his controlling.....

The poet Gerard Manley Hopkins was another who felt the presence of creative forces, especially when confronted with a courageous act, a scene of beauty or someone of fair countenance. It was as if the spectacle triggered off an inner response that led to his being creative himself.

On one occasion he was watching a bird fight its way against a high wind on a cliff-top. The bird was a windhover, a sort of falcon and it produced an instress in the visual patterns of his mind, thus "the instress of inscape" which led immediately to a spiritual experience of great ecstasy and inner effulgence. The perfection within him rushes out to meet the perfection, 'the achieve of, the mastery' of the bird.

*The Jewel in the Lotus, by the author (Baker Publications)

The Windhover

I caught this morning morning's minion, kingdom of daylight's
   dauphin, dapple-dawn-drawn Falcon, in his riding
   Of the rolling level underneath him steady air, and striding
High there, how he rung upon the rein of a wimpling wing
In his ecstasy! then off, off forth on swing,
   As a skate's heel sweeps smooth on a bow-bend: the hurl
     and gliding
   Rebuffed the big wind. My heart in hiding
Stirred for a bird - the achieve of, the mastery of the thing!
Brute beauty and valour and act, oh, air, pride, plume here
   Buckle! AND the fire that breaks from thee then, a billion
Times told lovelier, more dangerous, O my chevalier!
   No wonder of it; sheer plod makes plough down sillion
Shine, and blue-bleak embers, ah my dear,
   Fall, gall themselves, and gash gold-vermilion.

                — Gerard Manley Hopkins

This was the sort of impact which W.H. had on Richardson, but it was more sustained, reborn at every sight of his beloved.

Suddenly all the misery and frustration of his life was ended. The wasteland was ready for the spiritual waters of creativeness. The muse grew closer and closer. It was hardly distinguishable from the boy. Alchemy, to which he had so often alluded, was happening everywhere. The mounds of rolled scripts were changing before his eyes, into distinct plays, each more and more perfected. He was, at his highest level of attainment when drawing, he knew not what, from W.H. He was inspired and wrote plays for every mood. The stepladder of each day was mounted scene after scene, with the muse urging him on through his beloved:-

How can my muse want subject to invent
While thou dost breathe, that pour'st into my verse
Thine own sweet argument, too excellent
For every vulgar paper to rehearse?
O' give thyself the thanks, if aught in me
Worthy persusal stand against thy sight:
For who's so dumb that cannot write to thee,
When thou thyself dost give invention light;
Be thou the tenth Muse, ten times more in worth
Than those old nine which rhymers invocate;
And he that calls on thee, let him bring forth
Eternal numbers to outlive long date.
   If my slight Muse do please these curious days
   The pain be mine, but thine shall be the praise.

Sonnet 38

It is right that THE TEMPEST be placed last in the writings. It was the spiritual height of his ladder of consciousness and the only step above that play was into infinity with his sudden death.

Compare the lines from Sonnet 34:-

Ah, but those tears are pearl which thy love sheds,
And they are rich and ransom all ill deeds.

with those from THE TEMPEST (Act I, scene II):-

Those are pearls that were his eyes;
Nothing of him that doth fade
But doth suffer a sea-change
Into something rich and strange.....

The lines from the sonnet were written while the boy was near but those of THE TEMPEST were written while W.H. was at sea undergoing 'a sea-change.'

LOVE'S LABOUR LOST and some others of his plays show a lively interest in sonnets. Seven were woven into this play alone. We have already noted their influence on LUCRECE and VENUS AND ADONIS.

The sonnets proclaim, not only his love for W.H. but Richardson's developing certainty of his own immortality. They were an accompaniment to all he wrote in those last years. The comedy AS YOU LIKE IT, one of his best, has a link with Sonnet 15, in the opening lines:-

.....This huge stage presenteth nought but shows
Whereon the stars in secret influence do comment....

Compare with:-

All the world's a stage,
And all the men and women merely players.....

THE SONNETS reflect the intensity of feeling, the high and the low water marks. The winters of discontent during the time W.H. and Richardson were parted, the summers of intimacy, the autumns of maturity and the springs of constancy, are all in the sonnets and they are reflected therefrom into the plays. Most of Richardson's work was done during his magnificent obsession with William Hart. There is no intention here to cover old ground. The point made here is that the plays, far from being written well into the seventeenth Century, were finished, so far as Richardson was concerned by September of 1594.

VENUS AND ADONIS

That the boy had inspired this the first work that Richardson had published, there can be no doubt. Sonnet 53 not only shows this but, more than any of the sonnets, gives the exact feelings and intentions of the poet. It also contains in its very last line, the name of the boy:-

What is your substance, whereof are you made,
That millions of strange shadows on you tend?
Since every one hath, every one, one shade,
And you, but one, can every shadow lend.
Describe Adonis, and the counterfeit
Is poorly imitated after you:
On Helen's cheek all art of beauty set,
And you in Grecian tires are painted new:
Speak of the spring and foison of the year,
The one doth shadow of your beauty show,
The other as your bounty doth appear;
And you in every blessed shape we know.
 In all external grace you have some part,
 But you like none, none you, for constant heart.

A very early rendering of the name 'William' suggests the meaning, through 'Wilhelm' of constancy and thus William Hart, Mr. W.H. to whom the sonnets were dedicated.

Lines five and six say that Adonis has been fashioned out of the boy's image. The first four lines are difficult to understand unless they are read in association with the nature of the 'anima mundi'.* The suggestion is that the beauty of the boy's aura gilds everything about him, and the poet sees this.

The opening lines of VENUS AND ADONIS proclaim immediately the method adopted by the poet in the formulation of the word imagery of the poem. The poem concerns a boy, a youth more interested in other matters than the sexual expression of his, as yet, unripe masculinity. Venus is to be the seducer. The wooing is to be one-sided and the wooed very reluctant indeed. The responses of Adonis to the persistent advances of Venus merely reflect the shyness, reticence and even the shame of W.H. in his early associations with the poet:-

> Hunting he lov'd, but love he laughed to scorn;
> Sick-thoughted Venus makes amain unto him,
> And like a bold-faced suitor 'gins to woo him.

and later:-

> With this she seizeth on his sweating palm,
> The precedent of pith and livelihood
> And, trembling in her passion, calls it balm
> Earth's sovereign salve to do a goddess good:
> Being so enraged, desire doth lend her force
> Courageously to pluck him from his horse.
> Over one arm the lusty courser's rein,
> Under her other was the tender boy,
> Who blush'd and pouted in a dull disdain,
> With leaden appetite, unapt to toy;
>> She red and hot as coals of glowing fire,
>> He red for shame, but frosty in desire.

This is hardly the imagery one would normally anticipate from such an encounter between lovers, with the roles reversed. The wooing, despite the more mature nature of Venus, is, to put it mildly, unusual.

* See *Psychology of Discipleship* by the author (Baker Publications) pp. 155 & 180.

THE IDENTITY OF W.H.

W.H. were the initials of William Hart, a youth living in Stratford whom Richardson met in the middle 80's when the boy was not yet sixteen. In THE SONNETS he makes a play on both the surname and the first name of the boy. In Sonnet 53, we have the line:-

'And you in every blessed shape we know.'

The most blessed of shapes is the heart. We say accordingly 'Bless your heart' even as a form of thanks. We talk of 'The Sacred Heart'; we name churches after it (the most famous one in Paris); 'affairs of the heart,' 'the inner sanctum of the heart.' The home of the soul, the heart's delight etc., are phrases we use often. We use 'heart' to signify the central aspect of almost everything we know.....the heart of the atom, the heart and soul of the party, the heart of the forest, the heart of the nation. This was even more so in the language of the Elizabethans. 'Hearts of Oak' refers not only to their stout ships, built of oak, but to the hearts of the men who sailed in them.

The line could thus be read:-

And you, Hart, in every shape we know....

and it would be especially meaningful to the first four lines of the sonnet and even to subsequent lines as well.

But the poet repeats his name again, and this time, gives the full name:-

'But you like none, none you, for constant heart.'

The word 'constant' clinches the matter. William derives from the Anglo-Norman meaning 'resolute,' 'constant.' Thus 'constant heart' gives William Hart. From the same source 'William' derives from 'Wilhelm' meaning

Hart. From the same source 'William' derives from 'Wilhelm' meaning 'resolute helmet.' The line 'And you in Grecian tires are painted new' relates to his Christian name for this line describes a Grecian headdress. Thus, the Greek Adonis is transformed into the present boy William, and is so named.

It was W.H. who finally presented THE SONNETS, edited only by himself, for publication. He also put them into a certain order. This order was broken by the printers without reference to William Hart who had joined the navy by then and was abroad. The first sonnets are, however, in chronological order. They describe the initial wooing of the boy and some of them are contemporary to the writing of VENUS AND ADONIS. Both the latter and the sonnets were inspired by Richardson's love for W.H.

The extreme shyness of the youth necessitated a very careful approach by the wooer. There had to be no suggestion directly or indirectly that Richardson himself was trying to establish a relationship that was anything but mere concern for the boy's well-being. He chose the most relevant of all topics for a boy of that age which is narcissism* and gently, he then drew the boy's thoughts towards the implications of that condition begging him to have a thought for the rest of mankind:-

> Look in thy glass, and tell the face thou viewest
> Now is the time that face should form another;
> Whose fresh repair if now thou not renewest,
> Thou dost beguile the world, unbless some mother.
> For where is she so fair whose unear'd womb
> Disdains the tillage of thy husbandry?
> Or who is he so fond will be the tomb
> Or his self-love, to stop posterity?
> Thou art thy mother's glass, and she in thee
> Calls back the lovely April of her prime:
> So thou through windows of thine age shalt see,
> Despite of wrinkles, this thy golden time.
>> But if thou live, remember'd not to be,
>> Die single, and thine image dies with thee.

Sonnet 3

* see plate III

The same note is persisted with for some time allowing for reaction and adjustment to take place. There is no suggestion here that the method was planned or that there was any deceit on Richardson's part. At the very first, before true love had embraced either, it was natural to guide the lovely youth towards love-making and its natural outcome in a son by some willing maid. Perhaps Richardson, a shrewd judge of manliness soon realised that hetero-sexual love was not going to be a likely development. If this were so, he would later be proved wrong, for W.H. would end his days a father of two lusty sons. Soon, heart-felt, spontaneous effusions became mutual. No doubt there were desperate attempts of a much older person to hold the interest of a much younger. The 'Shakespearean' plays often warn of placing dependency on a boy's love. The true author of the sonnets is also aware of the dangers that accompany a narcissism that is dwelt upon or not healthily shaken off and in which boys may frequently indulge in:-

> Unthrifty loveliness, why dost thou spend
> Upon thyself thy beauty's legacy?
> Nauture's bequest gives nothing, but doth lend,
> And being frank, she lends to those are free.
> Then, beauteous niggard, why dost thou abuse
> The bounteous largess given thee to give?
> Profitless usurer, why dost thou use
> So great a sum of sums, yet canst not live?
> For having traffic with thyself alone,
> Thou of thyself thy sweet self dost deceive.
> Then how, when nature calls thee to be gone,
> What acceptable audit canst thou leave?
> > Thy unused beauty must be tomb'd with thee,
> > Which, used, lives th' executor to be.

Sonnet 4

In Sonnet 14, there is a subtle change. The boy is responding. There is not now that intense preoccupation with himself, the source of his basic shyness. He is beginning to look outwards and about him. Where now should he place his energies? Richardson now advises him to express those energies in truth and beauty, in such things as poetry, music, discourse and nature. Sublimation of energies is besought whereas the alternative is the death and waste of his potential:-

> Not from the stars do I my judgement pluck;
> And yet methinks I have astronomy,
> But not to tell of good or evil luck,
> Of plagues, or dearths, or season's quality;
> Nor can I fortune to brief minutes tell,
> Pointing to each his thunder, rain and wind,
> Or say with princes if it should go well,
> By oft predict that I in heaven find:
> But from thine eyes my knowledge I derive,
> And, constant stars, in them I read such art,
> As truth and beauty shall together thrive,
> If from thyself to store thou wouldst convert;
> > Or else of thee this I prognosticate:
> > Thy end is truth's and beauty's doom and date.

Sonnet 14

The shift here in implication is that the poet is feeding from the beauty and truth that emanates from the youth when he is chaste, 'not having traffic with thyself alone.' It is interesting that he stresses the output of the boy's eyes, likening them unto the stars themselves (from which flow astrological forces.) Even at this time, it is said the Russians are examining the outflow of energies from the eyes, the optic nerve being the only part of the brain that can be observed from the outside world (by looking at it through the eyes pupils) and when occult tradition has it that man's creative energies are trapped within the very works of art that he is creating.

The sentiment is taken further in the next sonnet which contains the whole meaning in the last few lines:-

> When I consider every thing that grows
> Holds in perfection but a little moment,
> That this huge stage presenteth nought but shows
> Whereon the stars in secret influence comment;
> When I perceive that men as plants increase,
> Cheered and check'd even by the self-same sky,
> Vaunt in their youthful sap, at height decrease,
> And wear their brave state out of memory;
> Then the conceit of this inconstant stay
> Sets you most rich in youth before my sight,
> Where wasteful Time debateth with Decay,
> To change your day of youth to sullied night;
>   And all in war with Time for love of you,
>   As he takes from you, I engraft you new.

Sonnet 15

This is the essence of immortality that he promises the boy in later sonnets and which he ensures (or thought he would ensure) in his dedication of the sonnets enshrined in the publisher's note, to the only begetter of them, Mr. W.H., to Mr. William Hart, his beloved. He says, pour out your loving energies to me now, when I am pressed so desperately for time and I will refurbish your inner nature, the eternal part of you with truth and beauty, even if you are not remembered for ever in the sonnets themselves.

A CLOSE THING

A CLOSE THING

*I*f there was ever going to be an exposè of the young Will Shakespeare, whose name was now beginning to be associated with an outpouring of highly successful plays, it would come from one who was likely to be at the pulse of current gossip or someone who had personal knowledge of the strange circumstances of a playwright who just would not come out into the open to receive the plaudits being showered on his works. There was one such candidate and his observations are with us today. If he had lived, the accuser would have been called to account for his apparently senseless attack on Shakespeare. Others, less involved with Shakespeare, had made attacks but had withdrawn them.

London was the centre, the very centre of social noise. It was also the heart of theatre land even in those early days as it remains to this day. When the plague struck at London in the early 90's the theatres were closed and the players forced to make a living in the distant counties. Stratford was always one of the most prized sites for the players and events in theatre there would soon filter back to the pamphleteers in London. Matters concerning a man in any prominent station in life would draw their attention, but those concerned with the theatre would be prized.

English, the language itself, as we know it today was in the melting pot. Its growth, like any language, depended on gossip tales, riddles and play on words, especially where these were tossed around in a central meeting place for them like London was. We have still the observation of pamphleteers of that time with us. Notable amongst these were Dekker, Peele, Kyd, and Nashe and a fifth named Robert Greene whom we met with earlier in these pages.

Unlike some of the pamphleteers, Greene had an academic background with, as we have already noted, a Master of Arts degree from Cambridge and also a degree from Oxford. His plays should have done well and he had aspirations to write in a literary style that would attract the most select readers and wealthy patrons. Unfortunately his best works, vigorous and forth-right were poorly promoted. Their lack of advancement had led to his being forced into writing pamphlets and plays and frequently, in both, he drew attention to the misdemeanours of society. His writings were sincere enough but the pressures of a dissolute life (something that Richardson dreaded,) forced him to become lax in his preparation and presentation of material for the London public whose intelligence he grossly underrated. Weak plots and poor characterisations began to reflect in audiences. Attendance at his plays fell. He became less sought after. His licentious living provoked his conscience and his later pamphlets were pointed at London's crime.

In February, 1592 Lord Strange's group of players opened their season in London at the Rose Theatre and the first play presented was a comedy by Robert Greene "Friar Bacon and Friar Bungay" and later in their busy season Greene's tragedy "Orlando Furioso" was also presented. Neither of these, or, for that matter, some other anonymous plays did well. But on Friday, March 3rd, a chronicle play HENRY THE SIXTH drew the largest audience of the season. The audiences did not know its author but certainly the world of dramatists knew that a young man called Will Shakespeare had offered the material for production.

It is easy for us to see how resentment arose in the mind of Robert Greene, but it was hard for the theatre-going public to account for his directing his spleen against Shakespeare. Greene openly professed a scorn for the stage and wrote plays only to provide means for his dissipated life.

He had reached the nadir of squalidness. His writings had been used and abused. The players had taken off into the provinces and with him went copies of his plays leaving him the squalor of flea-ridden circumstances in a London gripped by bubonic plague. He himself was dying.

In his last days he wrote a letter to his fellow dramatists drawing their attention to the way in which players were cashing in on author's efforts and abusing what we would call today copyright. In particular, he singled out Shakespeare and chose a line from the third part of HENRY VI to parody him:-

"O tigrer's heart wrapp'd in a woman's hide!"

Richard Plantagenet, Duke of York, addresses the words to Queen Margaret. Greene wrote:-

. . . . Yes trust them not : for there is an up-start Crow, beautified with our feathers, that with his Tyger's hart wrapt in a Player's hyde, supposes he is as well able to bombast out a blank vers as the best of you : and being an absolute Johannes factotum, is in his owne conceit the onely Shake-scene in a country. O that I might entreat your rare wits to be employed in more profitable courses : and let those Apes imitate your past excellence, and never more acquaint them with your admired inventions . . . . .

Especially young Shakespeare in his player's hide is also described as a jack-of-all-trades, implying that he is master of none, especially in terms of writing plays. That he is a 'Johannes factotum,' somebody who patches up, puts things together, was apt of Shakespeare, who before his reputation as a playwright became established, seems to have been employed in very small parts, menial tasks, and to have fulfilled many of the makeshift tasks demanded of a troupe including the handling of scenery, the patching of plays etc.

Why pick on Shakespeare? And why this particular line? It is no worse than many others in construction.

All critics generally agree that Shakespeare was no tiger in character.

The line implies that Shakespeare is only a player, nothing more. That Shakespeare is a 'shaker of scenes' and of scenery, doubly enforces the contention that he is not a playwright but a mere player. A man who knows he is dying (he died on September 2nd) is not likely to write such a serious letter for no reason except irritation over the success of somebody else's play. Greene had something to say that was important. He was well-placed, as we have noted, to have information on the truth about behind-the-scenes activities of a playwright, provincial or otherwise, who used a Shakespeare as a front man or agent to present his plays in the busy theatre land of London.

In fact, Greene had met Richardson in Oxford as we have noted and he knew why Richardson's plays were being passed on by Shakespeare. It galled him to think that a nonentity was getting credit for plays that were equalling, even surpassing his own.

"Tiger's heart" in the Elizabethan period was not as expressive, nor as popular as the term "lion-heart", but in parody it could well imply it for Richard the Lion Heart, England's most beloved king, was still a house-hold word and of the same stuff as the Chronicle Plays (including HENRY VI) were made of. The words `heart` and `sun` and "son" (and even `sonnet`) were often interchangeable in Elizabethan days as Sonnet 33 and Sonnet 24 give witness to.

A Close Thing

The first sonnet likens his love, the boy (Hart), to a sun and to a 'son of the world' which shone on him one morning:

Full many a glorious morning have I seen
Flatter the mountain tops with sovereign eye,
Kissing with golden-face the meadows green
Gilding pale streams with heavenly alchemy;
Anon permit the basest clouds to ride
With ugly rack on his celestial face,
And from the forlorn world his visage hide,
Stealing unseen to west with this disgrace.
Even so my sun one early morn did shine
With all-triumphant splendour on my brow;
But out, alack! he was but one hour mine,
The region cloud hath mask'd him from me now.
    Yet him for this my love no whit disdaineth;
    Suns of the world may stain when heaven's
        sun staineth.

In the next sonnet, sun, heart and hart are located in the bosom's shop:-

Mine eye hath play'd the painter and hath stell'd
Thy beauty's form in table of my heart;
My body is the frame wherein 'tis held,
And perspective it is best painter's art.
For through the painter must you see his skill,
To find where your true image pictur'd lies,
Which in my bosom's shop is hanging still,
That hath his windows glazed with thine eyes.
Now see what good turns eyes for eyes have done.
Mine eyes have drawn thy shape, and thine for me
Are windows to my breasts, where-through the sun
Delights to peep, to gaze therein on thee.
    Yet eyes this cunning want to grace their art,
    They draw but what they see, know not the
        heart.

Still, to this day, the name Richard is associated with the Lion Heart, and with this in mind, and the interchangeability of 'heart' with 'sun' or 'son', the implications of "Tiger's heart" in a player's hide, become clearer.

Greene KNEW the secret and respected Richardson's desire for anonymity but could not abide the thought that this 'upstart crow' would continue to cover himself with the feathers of a dramatist when he was nothing more than an indifferent actor of small parts, a callow youth from the shires.

Richard's son (heart) in a player's hide.

Sonnets were often circulated amongst close friends only or amongst those who were poetic. It is possible that Richardson showed Greene some of his sonnets because the link between 'lion' and 'tiger' is found in the first four lines of Sonnet 19 :-

> Devouring Time, blunt thou the lion's paws,
> And make the earth devour her own sweet brood;
> Pluck the keen teeth from the fierce tiger's jaw,
> And burn the long lived phoenix in her blood;
> Make glad and sorry seasons as thou fleet'st,
> And do whate'er thou wilt, shift-footed Time,
> To the wide world and all her fading sweets;
> But I forbid thee one most heinous crime:
> O, carve not with thy hours my love's fair brow,
> Nor draw no lines there with thine antique pen;
> Him in thy course untainted do allow
> For beauty's pattern to succeeding men.
>   Yet do thy worst, old Time: despite thy wrong,
>   My love shall in my verse ever live young.

There was already established in Richardson's plays, an association between King Richard the Lion Heart and a lion's hide. The Spanish Tragedy, first performed in 1589, may have influenced Richardson with these lines :-

> He hunted well that was a lion's death,
> Not he that in a garment wore his skin;
> So hares may pull dead lions by the beard.

Act I, Sc. I

These lines refer to the Duke of Austria wearing Richard Coeur de Lion's lion skin. In the play, KING JOHN, purported to be Shakespeare's are the lines :-

> You are the hare of whom the proverb goes,
> Whose valour plucks dead lions by the beard.

Act II Sc. I

In KING JOHN, Act III, Sc. I, this line is addressed to the Duke of Austria who is attempting to usurp the qualities of King Richard the Lion Heart by wearing his lion's hide:-

> Thou wear a lion's hide! Doff it for shame,
> And hang a calf's skin on those recreant limbs.

And who repeats this line twice more? Richard's son! Surely, no where in the whole outpouring of work attributed to Shakespeare, is there the repetition of any line THREE times.

Richard's son, three times calls a usurper wearing a hide to remove it. Surely all these accumulated factors are not just coincidence. To re-emphasise the matter, the son of Richard, in the last scene of the play, makes the final speech. Normally this honour is reserved for the character of highest rank, but here it is given to Richard's son, the only man in the play, it is generally agreed, fit to be king.

The speech that is made, is one of the most famous and the most stirring in the English language:-

> This England never did, nor ever shall,
> Lie at the proud foot of a conqueror,
> But when it first did help to wound itself.

> Come the three corners of the world to arms,
> And we shall shock them.

Richardson knew those lines would be quoted again and again if England ever went to war or was threatened from without. They are immortal and the character who speaks them is immortalised by them, Richard's son, and so too is Richardson.

Had Greene lived to survive Richardson, there is no doubt that Shakespeare's growing prominence would have come under further scrutiny and whether Greene would have continued to respect Richardson's desire for anonymity after his own death is doubtful. It was a close thing for Will Shakespeare. He was fortunate. Both Greene and Richardson were dead within two years.

There were others who knew the truth but we shall see how effectively Shakespeare dealt with them. One of them was William Hart (Mr. W.H.), and another was his own wife.

Plate I : Anne Hathaway's cottage

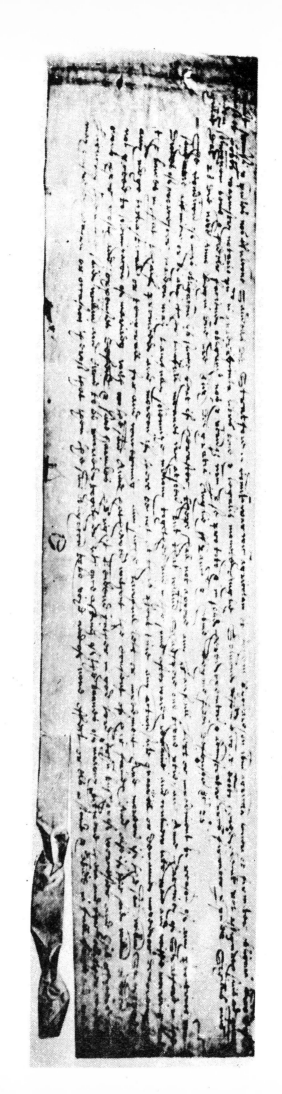

Plate II : With this document, John Richardson and his brother-in-law, Fulk Sandells, guaranteed the validity of William Shakespeare's proposed marriage to Anne Hathaway. (ref. page 42)

Plate III : Narcissus (ref. page 58-59)

Greenes

Sweet boy, might I aduise thee, be aduisde, and get not
many enemies by bitter wozdes : inueigh against vaine
men, foz thou canst do it, no man better, no man so well :
thou hast a libertie to repzooue all, and name none; foz
one being spoken to, all are offended; none being blamed
no man is iniured. Stop shallow water still running, it
will rage, oz tread on a wozme and it will turne : then
blame not Schollers vexed with sharpe lines, if they re-
pzoue thy too much liberty of repzoofe.

    And thou no lesse deseruing than the other two , in
some things rarer, in nothing inferiour ; dziuen (as my
selfe) to extreme shifts, a litle haue I to say to thee: and
were it not an idolatrous oth, I would sweare by sweet
S. Geozge, thou art vnwozthy better hap, sith thou de-
pendest on so meane a stay . Base minded men all thzee
of you, if by my miserie you be not warnd: foz vnto none
of you (like mee) sought those burres to cleaue : those
Puppets (I meane) that spake from our mouths, those
Anticks garnisht in our colours. Is it not strange, that
I, to whom they all haue beene beholding: is it not like
that you, to whome they all haue beene beholding, shall
(were yee in that case as I am now) bee both at once of
them fozsaken '? Yes trust them not : foz there is an vp-
start Crow, beautified with our feathers, that with his
Tygers hart wrapt in a Players hyde, supposes he is as
well able to bombast out a blanke verse as the best of
you : and beeing an absolute Iohannes fac totum, is in
his owne conceit the onely Shake-scene in a countrey.
O that I might intreat your rare wits to be imploied in
moze pzofitable courses : & let those Apes imitate your
past excellence, and neuer moze acquaint them with
your admired inuentions . I knowe the best husband of
                                    you

Plate 1V : Robert Green's attack on Shakespeare
Note the special treatment given to the line
'Tygers hart wrapt in a Players hyde.'

Plate V : Sir Philip Sydney (ref. page 78)

Plate VI:
Henry Wriothesley, Third Earl of Southampton (ref. page 75)

Plate VII : Mistress Mary Fitten (ref. page 89)

Plate VII: Shakespeare's Birthplace

Where W.H. later lived with Shakespeare's sister Joan, whom he had married.

Place IX: Above, gardens at New Place (ref. page 18 & 20)
Below left, Church of the Holy Trinity, Stratford.
Below right, bust of the bard therein.

Plate X: (ref. page 96)

Medallion of the poet George Chapman, famous for his vigorous translations of Homer. He featured in the life of W.H. but was never a serious contender for his affections. Died 1604.

MISTER W.H.

MISTER W.H.

𝕿HE SONNETS were dedicated to a Mr. W.H. whose identity has always presented a fascinating problem for study. The mystery arises from the terse dedication found in the 1609 Quarto which has been reproduced on page 103. Some believe it to be a typically worded dedication according to the bombastic style of the editor of the first edition of THE SONNETS i.e. Thomas Thorpe.

Today, most people accept that Mr. W.H. was the fair youth mentioned in most of the sonnets. The interpretation of the word 'begetter' as being the one who inspired the sonnets has led to the supposition that this was Henry Wriothesley, the 3rd Earl of Southampton, an aristocrat who was the patron of many Elizabethan writers. This concept assumes that the initials were reversed and that this boy, not a very attractive one, as the portrait shows *(see plate VI)* and to whom VENUS AND ADONIS, had been dedicated, was also the begetter of THE SONNETS.

In fact, the sonnets were addressed to William Hart, almost in their entirety. As Richardson lay dying in September 1594, he wrote the dedication and enclosed it, with the sonnet manuscripts, and gave the package to his wife Mary with the instruction that it was to be handed to William Hart on his return from abroad. Other instructions were also given with regard to the future publication of the plays.

If this book does nothing more than encourage further research into the lives of William Hart and John Richardson, it will have served its purpose. The volume that succeeds this one will be of help in this direction. The place of birth and the exact year of birth for William Hart is, as yet, unknown. The location of this piece of information could lead to a breakthrough in this whole subject. Sufficient is to record here that William Hart was not born in Stratford but in a town some miles away. The Harts moved to Stratford and started their business there. There were two brothers, presumably older than William, John and Michael.

The father was an artisan, probably a stone-mason. It was a family that kept much to themselves, having no pretensions to break out beyond their class and their own occupations. But William was different; he was an extremely sensitive youth. He blushed easily and was awkward in company. It was soon evident that he was not going to take kindly to being a hatter's apprentice. His brothers did not understand him and kept their distance. Richardson did business with the brothers in cartage contracting and it was there, at the hatter's shop in Stratford, owned by the two brothers that he first met William.

William Hart's natural shyness raised barriers when he met anyone. Richardson was everything that the youth was not. He was direct, blunt, to the point, forceful, unrelenting, decisive and pragmatic. Richardson was hard on the exterior and soft and warm beneath it all. William Hart was the opposite. His inordinate shyness and spells of flushing were often mentioned in THE SONNETS :-

> The forward violet thus did I chide:
> Sweet thief, whence did thou steal thy sweet that smells,
> If not from my love's breath? The purple pride
> Which on thy soft cheek for complexion dwells
> In my love's veins thou hast too grossly dyed.
> The lily I condemned for thy hand,
> And buds of marjoram had stol'n thy hair;
> The roses fearfully on thorns did stand,
> One blushing shame, another white despair;
> A third, nor red nor white, had stol'n of both,
> And to his robbery had annex'd thy breath;
> But, for his theft, in pride of all his growth
> A vengeful canker eat him up to death.
>> More flowers I noted, yet I none could see
>> But sweet or colour it had stol'n from thee.

Sonnet 99

Richardson made everything seem exciting to the boy. He could seize on any topic which William might faintly introduce and bring out the essence of it. John would lead the conversation into exhilarating paths that the boy had never heard of. William was never sorry when Richardson made a point of calling at the shop after he had got over the impact of first meeting him. The latter has such a knack of establishing rapport with him that William always felt like expressing his innermost thoughts. These were areas of himself that he dared not probe, and John would prize them out of him.

When players visited Stratford, they attended the shows together. John Richardson knew many of the actors personally and could describe, with incredible understanding, those parts of the play that were remote to the boy. William began to call at the house at Shottery and was reassured by the presence of John's large family. Mary Richardson was always distant but very kind. The children accepted him as one of the family. Mary never probed or showed resentment over the time the boy spent with her husband. William loved the free, intellectual atmosphere at Shottery, the browsing over manuscripts, the foul copies and increasingly made suggestions and even offered encouragement. He grew very perceptive and listened carefully to the information that Shakespeare gave as to the state of the theatre in London and how altering a script here and there could make its presentation a 'hit'. At first Hart had nothing to do with the financial dealings between John and Will Shakespeare but, inevitably, he became aware that the latter was the businessman and presenter and that John was too absorbed in the work of playwright.

Discussions would continue way into the night. Sometimes the visiting players were brought back to the house and were regaled with extracts from John's plays and were invited to give their comments. They also noted the presence of William Hart and understood something of Richardson's reasons for not moving up to London which was the site of the action.

The closeness of Richardson sometimes, at the very beginning of their association, sent W.H. scampering into himself. But John would sense this in an uncanny way and would leave him to recover. He was always glad when John returned, as if nothing had happened and without questions. They took long walks into the countryside around Shottery and would become en-thralled together over something of rare beauty. John would write some verse about it, making it exciting and the boy would reciprocate with a verse of his own. The youth grew unafraid and loved the way in which Richardson compared him, or part of him, to some quality of beauty or truth that had attracted them both to a scene in nature.

O, how much more doth beauty beauteous seem
By that sweet ornament which truth doth give!
The rose looks fair, but fairer we it deem
For that sweet odour which doth in it live.
The canker-blooms have full as deep a dye
As the perfumed tincture of the roses,
Hang on thorns, and play wantonly
When summer's breath their masked buds discloses:
But, for their virtue only is their show,
They live unwoo'd, and unrespected fade;
Die to themselves. Sweet roses do not so;
Of their sweet deaths are sweetest odours made:
    And so of you, beauteous and lovely youth,
    When that shall fade, by verse distils your truth.

Sonnet 54

It was not just vanity on the youth's part, not even self-love alone. It was as if he were on a voyage of discovery. John was the pilot and the hidden lands were his own nature that had been concealed within him till then. William was not surprised when the first sonnet was addressed to him. He knew that Richardson had greatly admired the soldier-poet Sir Philip Sidney *(see plate V)* and his sonnets. Sydney's sonnet sequence had been issued in an unauthorised publication about the time that John had met W.H. on the first occasion. But the boy was soon amazed at the plethora of verse that followed from Richardson's own pen. Hart was allowed to make copies of some and would shyly ask John to elaborate on obscure aspects of their meaning and allusions. The SONNETS however, were deeply personal, some so personal that, with John's consent, he destroyed them or asked for them to be re-phrased. He grew used to the names of endearment with which Richardson addressed him like 'My Sweet(hart),' and 'Constant One,' and another which we shall examine later. This subject, what to leave in the sonnet and what to take out, is captured herein:-

Mine eye and heart are at a mortal war,
How to divide the conquest of thy sight;
Mine eye my heart thy picture's sight would bar,
My heart mine eye the freedom of that right.
My heart doth plead that thou in him dost lie,
A closet never pierced with crystal eyes,
But the defendant doth that plea deny,
And says in him thy fair appearance lies.
To 'cide this title is empanelled
A quest of thoughts, all tenants to the heart;
And by their verdict is determined
The clear eye's moiety and the dear heart's part:
   As thus; mine eye's due is thine outward part,
   And my heart's right thine inward love of heart.

Sonnet 46

The reiteration of 'heart' seven times in this one sonnet is more than just extraordinary, it is a definite indication of something profound . . . . a pointer to the begetter of the sonnet.

W.H. was deeply aware of the transformation which the poet was effecting on him. It was not just the growth and integrating of his personality so that it could become expressive but there were spiritual qualities like insight into immortality, the sharing of high thoughts spontaneously and the factor of the 'soul' that intrigued him. Today, in the light of modern psychology, we would call these esoteric developments 'psychosynthesis'.*

---

* The raising of a point of consciousness to a higher level in the psyche and the reassembling of the personality around it.

William Hart paid tribute to his teacher and lover who was changing him so fast by writing him into his own sonnets, the several included with Richardson's own outpouring:-

> So oft have I invoked thee for my Muse
> And found such fair assistance in my verse
> As every alien pen hath got my use
> And under thee their poesy disperse.
> Thine eyes, that taught the dumb on high to sing
> And heavy ignorance aloft to fly,
> Have added feather's to the learned's wing
> And given grace a double majesty.
> Yet be most proud of that which I compile,
> Whose influence is thine and born of thee:
> In others' works thou dost but mend the style,
> And arts with thy sweet graces graced be;
>   But thou art all my art, and dost advance
>   As high as learning my rude ignorance.

Sonnet 78

Sonnet 79 is in chronological order and is Richardson's answer to the last one :-

> Whilst I alone did call upon thy aid,
> My verse alone had all thy gentle grace;
> But now my gracious numbers are decay'd
> And my sick Muse doth give another place.
> I grant, sweet love, thy lovely argument
> Deserves the travail of a worthier pen;
> Yet what of thee thy poet doth invent
> He robs thee of, and pays it thee again.
> He lends thee virtue, and he stole that word
> For thy behaviour; beauty doth he give,
> And found it in thy cheek: he can afford
> No praise to thee but what in thee doth live.
>   Then thank him not for that which he doth say,
>   Since what he owes thee thou thyself dost pay.

John taught W.H. to ride and the youth became an even more frequent visitor, riding over to Shottery where Richardson was always impatient to see him. There seemed no end to the latter's industry. Scroll after scroll fell from his pen. William helped where he could, sorting them carefully and then placing them in the wine barrel. The two would sit up half the night, long after the household had retired, talking and enthusing. Sometimes Mr. Shakespeare, back from London, would join them, bringing advice and news. John would always listen to Shakespeare whose advice he found invaluable. He also invited Hart's comments. Shakespeare suspected the relationship but never said anything. He respected Hart who had such a profound influence on Richardson, which he himself did not possess. He had noted that the whole quality and volume of Richardson's work had increased since he met William Hart. Shakespeare knew what the theatres were panting for. A suggestion here from him and a comment there from Hart and the manuscript in the hands of such a Johannes factotum became a fully fledged play. The matter of authorship was not yet important. Richardson still had no desire to leave Shottery and nor had W.H. at this stage.

Sometimes the energy of Richardson would wash into Hart and he began to experiment with the sonnet form himself. The deep feelings they felt for each other now showed outwardly as a camaraderie, one that was extended to others who called at Shottery. But the ardour of the older man for W.H. had no end. Hart was no longer shy, in his presence, at least. He even chided Richardson over his shortcomings and irascibility that so often failed to match up to the sentiments expressed in THE SONNETS.

Perhaps this is the best place to mention that Richardson had a drinking problem. It was at its worst during the writing of the Chronicle Plays where it reflected into the character of Falstaff. Indeed, he sometimes used the cowardly knight to cover for his drinking bouts. Falstaff was popular with the theatre-goers too and many reasons have been given for his character being extended into other plays. Richardson saw everything that was noble in Hart as being reflected in the qualities of Prince Hal. It was the emergence of Hart as a factor in his life that enabled him to forbear drinking and to spend all his energies on play writing. Nevertheless, the dread was always there that a relapse could occur. This factor is expressed best of all in the sonnet where Richardson castigates himself :-

> Alas 'tis true I have gone here and there,
> And made myself a motley to the view,
> Gored my own thoughts, sold cheap what is most dear,
> Made old offences of affections new;
> Most true it is that I have look'd on truth
> Askance and strangely: but, by all above,
> These blenches gave my heart another youth,
> And worse essays proved thee my best of love. . .

Sonnet 110

So long as W.H. was there, the writings kept coming in vaster and more fluent gushes. His absence brought brooding and pining with the possibilities that he, Richardson, would slip back into old ways :-

> Mine appetite I never more will grind
> On newer proof,* to try and older friend,
> A god in love, to whom I am confined.

In all these circumstances, John Richardson's denial of fame, by remaining ensconced in Shottery and using Shakespeare as his agent, is understandable. He did not want to revert to old ways and he did not want Hart subjected to the kind of atmosphere that abiding in London would ensure.

Hart, himself, loved the theatre but could not stand the very same pseudo-aestheticism that still frequently marks the social and professional tenure of theatre today, the relationships between men and men, the petty intrigues, the scandals, needless effeminacy and the insincerity. He could not cope with it outside of the mild intrusions it presented at Shottery when players called. Hart made it clear to Richardson that whilst he understood these things went on and were even a necessary part of proceedings, they were not for him and nor was that part of London for him.

---

* 'proof' here may well be taken as referring to alcoholic strength.

Richardson was glad. Nothing suited him better than for the youth to remain free from it all. To hell with London. Let Shakespeare get on with the business side of things and who cared about authorship anyway. He did not realise that theatre was gaining such ground in the hearts of the people that authorship would soon become the mark of much greater respect, and of fame, in their eyes.

Some say THE SONNETS are sugary and use the words 'sweet' and 'heart' excessively but with the identity of W.H. established such sonnets as number 47 become more meaningful. Note that Richardson, in the first line, describes himself as being a league from heart which was the distance between his home in Shottery where the sonnet was being written and Hart at their shop in Stratford:-

> Betwixt mine eye and heart a league is took,
> And each doth good turns now unto the other:
> When that mine eye is famish'd for a look,
> Or heart in love with sighs himself doth smother,
> With my love's picture then my eye doth feast
> And to the painted banquet bids my heart;
> Another time mine eye is my heart's guest
> And in his thoughts of love doth share a part:
> So, either by the picture or my love,
> Thyself away art present still with me;
> For thou not farther than my thoughts canst move,
> And I am still with them and they with thee;
>   Or, if they sleep, thy picture in my sight
>   Awakes my heart to heart's and eye's delight.

'Sweet' refers not only to the poet's sweetheart (Hart), but to 'Sweet William' (Hart), a flower of the English countryside that grows so prolifically around Stratford. The phrase 'thy budding name' then becomes more meaningful. Thus, W.H. had, through his Christian and his surnames subject matter to relate them to common flowers :-

How sweet and lovely dost thou make the shame
Which, like a canker in the fragrant rose,
Doth spot the beauty of thy budding name!
O, in what sweets dost thou thy sins enclose!
That tongue that tells the story of thy days,
Making lascivious comments on thy sport,
Cannot dispraise but in a kind of praise;
Naming thy name blesses an ill report.
O, what a mansion have those vices got
Which for their habitation chose out thee,
Where beauty's veil doth cover every blot
And all things turn to fair that eyes can see!
    Take heed, dear heart; of this large privilege;
    The hardest knife ill used doth lose his edge.

Sonnet 95

In this last sonnet there are indications that the relationship of the older man and the youth arouses comment and scandal. In the absence of stupidity, one can only assume that those who describe the friendship between the poet and W.H. as being entirely platonic, are being downright dishonest. That relationship could not be more unequivocally described than in Sonnet 20:-

A woman's face with nature's own hand painted
Hast thou, the master-mistress of my passion;
A woman's gentle heart, but not acquainted
With shifting change, as is false women's fashion;
An eye more bright than their's, less false in rolling,
Gilding the object whereupon it gazeth;
A man in hue, all 'hues' in his controlling,
Which steals men's eyes and women's souls amazeth.
And for a woman wert thou first created;
Till Nature, as she wrought thee, fell a-doting,
And by addition me of thee defeated,
By adding one thing to my purpose nothing,
    But since she prick'd thee out for women's pleasure,
    Mine be thy love, and thy love's use their treasure.

The seventh line of the sonnet excited Oscar Wilde who believed this to indicate a relationship between the poet and one of the young actors. In fact, the word 'hue' is used in connection with noisy words, e.g. 'hue and cry'. The sonnet is meant to comfort the youth who is the target of scandal being circulated by one of his friends, probably named 'Hugh.'

> Your love and pity doth the impression fill
> Which vulgar scandal stamp'd upon my brow;
> For what care I who calls me well or ill,
> So you o'er-green my bad, my good allow?
> You are my all the world, and I must strive
> To know my shames and praises from your tongue;
> None else to me, nor I to none alive,
> That my steel'd sense or changes right or wrong.
> In so profound abyss I throw all care
> Of others' voices, that my adder's sense
> To critic and to flatterer stopped are.
> Mark how with my neglect I do dispense:
>> You are so strongly in my purpose bred
>> That all the world besides methinks are dead.

Sonnet 112

Richardson was able to manage scandal without submitting to the same emotional responses which it evoked in W.H. Richardson acted out his discomfort within himself, in his sonnets, in his plays, and, very infrequently in drinking. Only W.H. could salve his wounds and keep him writing. The last line of the next sonnet tells why he would not go up to London and assume his crown as monarch of playwrights. He preferred to ignore the world of theatre and sink himself into his work and into the relationship established with W.H.

When, in disgrace with fortune and men's eyes,
I all alone beweep my outcast state,
And trouble deaf heaven with my bootless cries,
And look upon myself, and curse my fate,
Wishing me like to one more rich in hope,
Featured like him, like him with friends possess'd
Desiring this man's art and that man's scope,
With what I most enjoy contented least;
Yet in these thoughts myself almost despising,
Haply I think on thee, and then my state,
Like to the lark at break of day arising
From sullen earth, sings hymns at heaven's gate;
    For thy sweet love remember'd such wealth brings
    That then I scorn to change my state with kings.

Sonnet 29

THE DARK LADY

THE DARK LADY

$\mathcal{S}$ome of the sonnets are said to refer to a woman who was the mistress of the poet who had written THE SONNETS. Some say she interfered with a relationship that existed between the poet and W.H. Others claimed there were two women; one even claimed that the Dark Lady of Sonnet 30 was Queen Elizabeth! Others said she was a negress, a courtesan etc. Lately, it has been Mistress Mary Fitton* *(see plate VII)* and who knows what it will be tomorrow.

*The identification of Mistress Mary Fitton with the Dark Lady has of late been accepted by many reliable historians. Her claims were first advanced by Thomas Tyler, in a paper read before the New Shakespeare Society at its meeting on May 30, 1884, and defended in his The Herbert-Fitton theory of Shakespeare's Sonnets (1898). Those who accept Pembroke as the young aristocrat (see Mr. W.H.) to whom Shakespeare addressed his sonnets find that the known facts of Mary Fitton's career as a maid of honour at the queens' court correspond to what Shakespeare tells us in the sonnets about the Dark Lady. (The Sonnets, New Variorum Edition, Hyder Rollins, ed., 1944.)

Other attempts at identification have included the name of Mrs. Jane Davenant, the wife of an Oxford vintner, who with her husband John kept the tavern at Oxford where Shakespeare is supposed to have put up with his frequent trips between London and Stratford. This identification was accepted and developed by Arthur Acheson in his Mrs. Davenant, the Dark Lady of Shakespeare's Sonnets (1913). In other books Acheson "discovered" that the Avisa of Willobie His Avisa (1594) was the Dark Lady and that she was Jane Davenant, the mother of an illegitimate son, Sir William Davenant, or whom Shakespeare was the father. According to John Aubrey, Sir William "seemed contented enough to be thought his (Shakespeare's) son." Indeed he took pains to spread the legend abroad. Acheson later made another discovery, that the distinction belonged not to Jane but to a supposititious Anne, John Davenant's first wife. But there is no proof that such a woman existed. She is apparently the figment of Acheson's imagination. (A Shakespeare Encyclopaedia, edited by Oscar James Campbell, Methuen & Co., Ltd., London.)

I must confess that in my researches into this matter, I entered many blind alleys myself and even came up with the Dark Lady being The Black Death or plague, whose kiss ravaged the cities of Europe during the period that THE SONNETS were written.

But the answer was simpler. It poses no contradictions to the content of THE SONNETS, no 'eternal triangle' of tangled love, no need to search into non-existent histories and genealogical trees. I felt as foolish as anyone who has speculated with the millions for four hundred years about the identity of the Dark Lady only to have it contradicted by THE SONNETS themselves. Anyone who has read them knows that the solution lies within them and not in some unrelated, outside factor. The answer to my search came, along with the main content of this book, from the same sources described in my opening pages. It may appal the romantics and dismay the scholars, but I will defy anyone, when he re-reads THE SONNETS, the proposition out-of-hand that, Richardson, at some great cost, purchased a lovely black filly for the youth. Her name was 'Black Beauty' and she was the Dark Lady.

Her taking ways, her tantrums, the bruises she inflicted, the falls, the delight she evoked, the rolling eyes and even the youth's preoccupation with her to the exclusion of Richardson, form the basis of some of the most contentious sonnets :-

> My mistress' eyes are nothing like the sun;
> Coral is far more red than her lips' red:
> If snow be white, why then her breasts are dun;
> If hairs be wires, black wires grow on her head.
> I have seen roses damask'd red and white,
> But no such roses see I in her cheeks;
> And in some perfumes is there more delight
> Than in the breath from my mistress reeks.
> I love to hear her speak, yet well I know
> That music hath a far more pleasing sound:
> I grant I never saw a goddess go,
> My mistress, when she walks, treads on the ground:
>> And yet, by heaven, I think my love as rare
>> As any she belied with false compare.

Sonnet 130

HOLLYHOCK by George Stubbs

Reproduced by gracious permission of Her Majesty the Queen

Now surely, this is no description of Miss Mary Fitton, no matter how fragmentary our real knowledge of her nature. It can't really describe a lady of the court, or one from the outer world, cruel as it is. The Dark Lady is portrayed on the previous page. Richardson was fascinated with horses and was pleased that Hart loved this one too. It would be strange if THE SONNETS which reflected life at Shottery did not include references to such an important event as the giving of a gift to his beloved. The Dark Lady comes up again in Sonnet 141 and in excellent chronological order. Note also that the owner of the filly, a youth called 'Hart' is mentioned THREE TIMES in this same sonnet.

> In faith, I do not love thee with mine eyes,
> For they in thee a thousand errors note;
> But 'tis my heart that loves what they despise,
> Who, in despite of view, is pleased to dote;
> Nor are mine ears with thy tongue's tune delighted;
> Nor tender feeling, to base touches prone,
> Nor taste, nor smell, desire to be invited
> To any sensual feast with thee alone:
> But my five wits nor my five senses can
> Dissuade one foolish heart from serving thee,
> Who leaves unsway'd the likeness of a man,
> Thy proud heart's slave and vassal wretch to be:
>   Only my plague thus far I count my gain,
>   That she that makes me sin awards me pain.

Sonnet 141

The last two lines indicate that the horse causes the poet to swear (and to sin). For this he pays with the pain of bruises from being thrown by the filly.

The youth himself does not escape the tyrannous conduct of the horse and Sonnet 133 playfully describes Hart's suffering and names Hart and 'heart' FIVE TIMES :-

> Beshrew that heart that makes my heart to groan
> For that deep wound it gives my friend and me!
> Is't not enough to torture me alone,
> But slave to slavery my sweet'st friend must be?
> Me from myself thy cruel eye has taken,
> And my next self thou harder hast engrossed:
> Of him, myself, and thee, I am forsaken;
> A torment thrice threefold thus to be crossed.
> Prison my heart in thy steel bosom's ward,
> But then my friend's heart let my poor heart bail;
> Who'er keeps me, let my heart be his guard;
> Thou can'st not then use rigour in my goal:
>> And yet thou wilt; for I, being pent in thee,
>> Perforce am thine, and all that is in me.

The line 'Prison my heart in thy steel bosom's ward' refers to the steel harness in which the filly is 'gaoled' but also to the fact that the horse dominates the boy's attention and whilst he rides her, he lies within the same steel gaol.

The tyranny which the filly maintains over the attention of W.H. is described in Sonnet 131 :-

> Thou art as tyrannous, so as thou art,
> As those whose beauties proudly make them cruel;
> For well thou know'st to my dear doting heart
> Thou art the fairest and most precious jewel.
> Yet, in good faith, some say that thee behold,
> Thy face hath not the power to make love groan:
> To say they err I dare not be so bold,
> Although I swear it to my self alone.
> And to be sure that is not false I swear,
> A thousand groans, but thinking on thy face,
> One on another's neck, do witness bear
> Thy black is fairest in my judgement's place.
>> In nothing art thou black save in thy deeds,
>> And thence this slander, as I think, proceeds.

The sonnet describes a black filly called 'Black Beauty' by whom the youth Hart is dominated, in that he dotes on her. 'One on another's neck' refers to his relationship with her out riding and under speed.

In Sonnet 132 he describes the soulful appearance of Black Beauty's eyes and compares each of them to an evening star. The name of the horse is given in the second to last line :-

'Then will I swear that Beauty herself is black.'

Thine eyes I love, and they, as pitying me,
Knowing they heart torments me with disdain,
Have put on black and loving mourners be,
Looking with pretty ruth upon my pain.
And truly not the morning sun of heaven
Better becomes the grey cheeks of the east,
Nor that full star that ushers in the even
Doth half that glory to the sober west,
As those two mourning eyes become they face:
O, let it then as well beseem thy heart
To mourn for me, since mourning doth thee grace,
And suit thy pity like in every part.
    Then will I swear beauty herself is black,
    And all they foul that thy complexion lack.

It was a joke at first for both Richardson and William Hart to address poems to their common mistress in that the former had purchased her and in that the latter had helped with the purchase and now possessed her affections. It was no deliberate red herring as some have written. There was nothing that could be described as 'devious' in THE SONNETS. They described almost entirely the relationship between the poet and the youth and anything associated with both of them. The cluster of sonnets described above which related to the filly, were in almost perfect chronological order. There was no court intrigue involved, or reference to the reigning monarch, no arch cover-up, no political implication intended. No doubt, some of the sonnets addressed to their equine mistress were deliberately released amongst the 'inner circle' of their friends. Some may have filtered through to the

Shakespeare circle, but they were never created as a device for such purposes. There was never any lady, as a source of contention between Richardson and W.H. That another poet attracted the youth, we all know to be true, and that this was almost certainly Chapman *(see plates)* but there was never any serious liaison between W.H. and another.

As the coup de grace in this revelation let us consider HENRY V, Act III, Sc. VII :-

Con. of France.	Indeed, my lord, it is a most absolute and excellent horse.....
Duke of Burbon.	.....I once writ a sonnet in his praise, and began thus: 'Wonder of nature,'—
Duke of Orleans.	I have heard a sonnet begin so to one's mistress.
Duke of Burbon.	Then did they imitate that which I composed to my courser; for my horse is my mistress.

Richardson and W.H. did not call the horse Black Beauty. That was the name it was bought under. They used a more endearing name; it was 'Love,' in fact pronounced by them 'lovee'. The following sonnet gives witness to this statement. It is a sonnet that has never been adequately explained by scholars and, for the life of me, such an explanation could only be forthcoming on the assumption that the words quoted in the sonnet refer to the sounds made by the horse when it whinnies and neighs :-

Those lips that Love's own hand did make
Breathed forth the sound that said 'I hate,'
To me that languish'd for her sake:
But when she saw my woeful state,
Straight in her heart did mercy come,
Chiding that tongue that ever sweet
Was used in giving gentle doom;
And taught it thus anew to greet;
'I hate' she alter'd with an end,
That follow'd it as gentle day
Doth follow night, who, like a fiend,
From heaven to hell is flown away;
    'I hate' from hate away she threw,
    And saved my life, saying 'not you'.

The poet had been thrown by the horse after one such neigh when she could easily have stamped on him but did not. The quote 'not you' refers to this action but to a change in the tone of the horse's neigh. Perhaps 'not you' is a subtle play on the words so that 'not you' and 'neigh' and 'nay' are all implied.

The author shall be accused of de-romanticising THE SONNETS by referring to the allegedly most erotic of them all which points also to the filly they had together named 'Lovee':-

Love is too young to know what conscience is;
Yet who knows not conscience is born of love?
Then, gentle cheater, urge not my amiss,
Lest guilty of my faults thy sweet self prove:
For, thou betraying me, I do betray
My nobler part to my gross body's treason;
My soul doth tell my body that he may
Triumph in love; flesh stays no farther reason,
But rising at thy name doth point out thee
As his triumph prize. Proud of this pride,
He is contented thy poor drudge to be,
To stand in thy affairs, fall by thy side.
No want of conscience hold it that I call
Her 'love' for whose dear love I rise and fall.

Sonnet 151

W.H. offered the sonnet above as his own to Richardson in support of the filly who has been responsible for bruisings all round. The erotic last line merely describes the rider's action on the back of his horse 'Love.'

In Sonnet 135, W.H. tenders another sonnet about the filly, making a play on his own name William or Will :-

> Whoever hath her wish, thou hast thy 'Will,'
> And 'Will' to boot, and 'Will' in over plus;
> More than enough am I that vex thee still,
> To thy sweet will making addition thus.
> Wilt thou, whose will is large and spacious,
> Not once vouchsafe to hide my will in thine?
> Shall will in others seem right gracious,
> And in my will no fair acceptance shine?
> The sea, all water, yet receives rain still,
> And in abundance addeth to his store;
> So thou, being rich in 'Will,' add to thy 'Will'
> One will of mine, to make thy large 'Will' more.
> > Let no unkind, no fair beseechers kill;
> > Think all but one, and me in that one 'Will.'

Richardson had to pay a lot of money for the horse and is also aware that she will occupy much of W.H.'s time to his own loss. Both he and Hart had to offer some security until the creature was paid for. This is used as the basic theme for the next sonnet which describes the bondage which the boy and the poet have entered into on her behalf:-

> So, now I have confess'd that he is thine
> And I myself am mortgaged to thy will,
> Myself I'll forfeit, so that other mine
> Thou wilt restore, to be my comfort still:
> But thou wilt not, nor he will not be free
> For thou art covetous and he is kind;
> He learn'd but surety-like to write for me,
> Under that bond that him as fast doth bind.
> The statute of thy beauty thou wilt take,
> Thou usurer, that put'st forth all to use,
> And sue a friend came debtor for my sake;
> So him I lose through my unkind abuse.
> > Him have I lost; thou hast both him and me:
> > He pays the whole, and yet am I not free.

> Sonnet 134

The Dark Lady

In Sonnet 41 the poet complains that Black Beauty has tempted the youth, womanlike, and through his loyalties to her, he is playing the poet false.

> Those pretty wrongs that liberty commits,
> When I am sometime absent from thy heart,
> Thy beauty and thy years full well befits,
> For still temptation follows where thou art.
> Gentle thou art, and therefore to be won,
> Beauteous thou art, therefore to be assailed;
> And when a woman woos, what woman's son
> Will sourly leave her till she hath prevailed?
> Ay me! but yet thou mightest my seat forbear,
> And chide thy beauty and thy straying youth,
> Who lead thee in their riot even there
> Where thou art forced to break a twofold truth,
>   Hers, by thy beauty tempting her to thee,
>   Thine, by thy beauty being false to me.

THE SONNETS
and their Dedication

The Sonnets and their Dedication

Examined objectively, part by part, and as a whole, the Dedication shows clearly the poet's final intention for THE SONNETS, his attitude towards their impetus and their inspiration, and the specific occasion which provoked the dedication :-

TO . THE . ONLIE . BEGETTER .
OF.
THESE . INSVING . SONNETS.
Mr. W . H . ALL . HAPPINESSE.
AND . THAT . ETERNITE.
PROMISED.
BY
OVR . EVER . LIVING . POET.
WISHETH.
THE . WELL-WISHING.
ADVENTVRER . IN.
SETTING.
FORTH.

T. T.

The 'onlie begetter,' the single inspirational force responsible for the intense outpouring of sentiment is stated clearly, a person who is male and who has the initials W.H. There is nothing equivocal about this. A man, and only recently a youth, with these initials, in close proximity to Stratford, associated with families that surrounded the writing of the plays and THE SONNETS is Mr. William Hart, who later, married into the Shakespeare family. The poet says W.H. is the only begetter and one would expect that begetter to figure prominently in THE SONNETS, either by direct reference, through naming, or indirectly through his qualities. If it is William Hart, then again, his name is more prominently repeated than any other, in places, seven times in one sonnet. Even the allusions to him constantly express matters pertaining to both his Christian and surname. This book has shown up these allusions as they pertained to features of daily life shared by the poet and his lover. It has also given far more adequate explanations pertaining to hitherto 'grey' areas of clarity of meaning, especially as regards the sonnets linked to 'The Dark Lady.' It has also been shown that W.H. wrote some of THE SONNETS and in this respect, he would again qualify for 'onlie begetter.'

Practically every sonnet is imprinted with the youth's effect on Richardson; he was the 'lark at break of day arising;' the sun which shines with 'all-triumphant splendour,' and also the one for whom a description of Adonis is a poor imitation and counterfeit of himself:-

> How can my Muse want subject to invent
> Whilst thou dost breathe, that pourest into my verse
> Thine own sweet argument?.....
> Be thou the tenth muse, ten times more in worth
> Than those old nine which rhymers invocate....

(from Sonnet 138.)

Through the help of a mutual friend with connections in the navy, W.H. is able to secure a post which will take him away from Stratford for some time. He is unaware that his old friend's health is in a very poor state, or that his very leaving, even if only temporary, would end Richardson's life. He calls on Richardson at Shottery to bid him a fond farewell, excited as any young man would be at the prospect of new experience and grateful to his friend for the help given to secure the naval position. His good wishes to John Richardson as he waves good-bye from his horse make, quite naturally, a lasting impression on the dying poet.

Reciprocally, the youth is wished 'all happiness' and in the dedication, the 'setting forth' of W.H. is recorded for all time and becomes part of 'that eternitie promised by our ever-living poet' to the one who had initiated THE SONNETS in the first place:-

> Yet do thy worst, Old Time! Despite thy wrong
> My love shall in my verse ever live young.

And again in Sonnet 18 :-

> Nor shall Death brag thou wander'st in his shade,
> When in eternal lines to time thou grow'st
> So long as men can breathe, or eyes can see
> So long lives this, and this gives life to thee.

That it was Richardson's intention to make W.H. immortal was clear from the first sonnets but even in Sonnet 81, it is written:-

> Or I shall live your epitaph to make,
> Or you survive when I in earth am rotten;
> From hence your memory death cannot take,
> Although in me each part will be forgotten.
> Your name from hence immortal life shall have,
> Though I, once gone, to all the world must die:
> The earth can yield me but a common grave,
> When you entombed in men's eyes shall lie.
> Your monument shall be my gentle verse,
> Which eyes not yet created shall o'er-read;
> And tongues to be your being shall rehearse,
> When all the breathers of this world are dead;
> > You shall live - such virtue hath my pen -
> > Where breath most breathes, even in the mouths of men.

When W.H. left, as the Dedication indicates, Richardson, aware of his approaching fate, collected THE SONNETS together for their rightful owner. He put his own final touches to these intense testaments of his love and admiration and made sure that his own identity and that of his beloved were in them for those who have the eyes to see.

W.H. had already left Stratford when the next sonnet was written;-

> No longer mourn for me when I am dead
> Than you shall hear the surly sullen bell
> Give warning to the world that I am fled
> From this vile world, with vilest worms to dwell:
> Nay, if you read this line, remember not
> The hand that writ it; for I love you so,
> That I in your sweet thoughts would be forgot,
> If thinking on me then should make you woe.
> O, if, I say, you look upon this verse
> When I perhaps compounded am with clay,
> Do not so much as my poor name rehearse,
> But let your love even with my life decay;
> > Lest the wise world should look into your moan,
> > And mock you with me after I am gone
>
> Sonnet 71

Concerning earlier investigations or theories about the identity of the boy in THE SONNETS and Mr. W.H. of the Dedication, Ivor Brown has this to say:-

> The Sonnet Mystery remains and will remain. Unless new facts are discovered, which is unlikely, there can be nothing but conjecture as to the persons and events behind these uneven but often superb outpourings of a spirit more often tormented than at peace.*

*Shakespeare, Ivor Brown, p.182

What seems unlikely, has become a reality in this book. We move into a new age wherein vastly new methods of research are available, some of them psychological, some of them even morphogenetic. The author is one of those unusual people who believes that no record of human events is entirely lost and that it is only a matter of time before techniques are evolved for recovering facts from the past. A grooved pot impressed by the style of some ancient potter might one day recall, through instrumentation, the sounds of what occurred in the pottery, when the pot was being thrown. The light of the stars could bring us information about those stars, had we sophisticated ways to apprehend it, dating back a million light years. We are already able to measure the background radiation of events that occurred simultaneously with 'the Big Bang' at the moment of the creation of the universe 15 billion years ago. Great areas of the human brain lie 'silent' awaiting function as Man evolves. Who is to say that knowledge, at least in part, from a period of a mere 400 years ago may not be recovered through unfoldment of such areas of the brain, or by new methods of psychological analysis and regression.

It may not add too much weight to the author's propositions but it is comforting for him to know that Sir Lawrence Olivier read the first edition of this work and considered the matter of the Dark Lady, thereafter 'solved'. He thought it a better explanation than any he had previously heard.

There is one more important factor to emphasise before this volume is complete. THE SONNETS suggest a great disparity in age between poet and youth. At the time in which it is generally agreed THE SONNETS were written, the poet would have been, if he were Shakespeare, less than thirty years of age. Let the reader decide whether, Sonnet 73 describes a man of thirty :-

> That time of year thou mayst in me behold
> When yellow leaves, or none, or few, do hang
> Upon those boughs which shake against the cold,
> Bare run'd choirs, where late the sweet birds sang.
> In me thou see'st the twilight of such day
> As after sunset fadeth in the west;
> Which by and by black night doth take away,
> Death's second self, that seals up all in rest,
> In me thou see'st the glowing of such fire,
> That on the ashes of his youth doth lie,
> As the death-bed whereon it must expire,
> Consumed with that which it was nourishe'd by.
> This thou perceivest, which makes thy love more strong,
> To love that well which thou must leave ere long.

Richardson was ten years older than Shakespeare, about forty when this sonnet was written.

INDEX

INDEX TO FIRST LINES OF SONNETS

INTRODUCTORY LINES

Convent garden

Somerset h.   Arundel house   Essex house